CHINA MATTERS

PRAISE FOR *CHINA MATTERS*

'For all its modern gloss, China is scarcely less strangely and severely governed by today's communist elite than it was under imperial dynasties. Yet its connections and influence have already become ubiquitous in Australia today, bringing great opportunity but also risk. This should command the educated attention of all Australians. That is why China matters. That is why *China Matters* matters.' —**Rowan Callick, author of** *Party Time: Who Runs China and How*

'Australians must learn to live with China's power. This is simply the best all-round guide we have for how to do this.' —**Hugh White, author of** *The China Choice: Why America Should Share Power*

'*China Matters* cuts through the volatile mix of hype, hysteria and complacency surrounding the Middle Kingdom in Australia to sketch out a nuanced road map for dealing with Asia's rising super power. Sober in tone, the book is really a wake-up call for Australians to recognise China and its ruling party for what they are, not as we would like them to be, and prepare accordingly.' —**Richard McGregor, author of** *The Party: The Secret World of China's Communist Rulers*

'For an Australia increasingly divided between a reliance on China for its future prosperity, and an apprehension about what a powerful China means for its security and values, *China Matters* is a timely intervention. Deeply knowledgeable, engagingly argued, and most importantly wise and balanced, this book should be read by all Australians who think seriously about their country's future.' —**Michael Wesley, author of** *Restless Continent: Wealth, Rivalry and Asia's New Geopolitics*

'Jakobson and Gill avoid the common twin traps of China analysis. They are not romantic or rabid. They offer a timely realism. This book helps brace Australia for a tricky future with a great, rising power that we need to understand.' —**Peter Hartcher, author of** *The Sweet Spot: How Australia Made Its Own Luck – And Could Now Throw It All Away*

CHINA MATTERS

GETTING IT RIGHT FOR AUSTRALIA

WHAT WE NEED TO KNOW – FOR TODAY AND TOMORROW

BATES GILL & LINDA JAKOBSON

LA TROBE
UNIVERSITY PRESS

IN CONJUNCTION WITH BLACK INC.

For Sarah

For Chris

Published by La Trobe University Press in conjunction with Black Inc.
Level 1, 221 Drummond Street
Carlton VIC 3053, Australia
enquiries@blackincbooks.com
www.blackincbooks.com
www.latrobeuniversitypress.com.au

National Library of Australia Cataloguing-in-Publication entry:

Gill, Bates author.
China matters: getting it right for Australia / Bates
Gill, Linda Jakobson.
9781863959179 (paperback)
9781925435542 (ebook)
Economic development–Social aspects–China.
China–Foreign economic relations–Australia.
China–Economic policy.
China–Economic conditions.
Jakobson, Linda, author.

Cover design by Peter Long
Text design and typesetting by Tristan Main
Cover image by Chuyuss, Shutterstock

Printed in Australia by McPherson's Printing Group.

FSC
www.fsc.org
MIX
Paper from
responsible sources
FSC® C001695

CONTENTS

ACKNOWLEDGEMENTS vii

ACRONYMS AND ABBREVIATIONS x

INTRODUCTION: Why this book? 1
Bates Gill and Linda Jakobson

1. THE CHINA DREAM: Return of the
Middle Kingdom 15
Linda Jakobson

2. SOCIAL CHANGE: Will the political
fabric unravel? 32
Linda Jakobson

3. CHINA'S ECONOMIC TRANSITION:
Will it succeed? 62
Arthur R. Kroeber

4. THE SOFT SIDE OF CHINESE POWER:
Projecting influence abroad 93
Bates Gill

5. CHINESE HARD POWER: How will
    China use its growing strength?   126
    Bates Gill

6. GETTING IT RIGHT FOR AUSTRALIA   160
    Bates Gill and Linda Jakobson

    ENDNOTES   193

    INDEX   203

Acknowledgements

Our first word of gratitude goes to each other. Co-authoring a book is akin to embarking on a journey together – one plans, one explores, one reflects. The journey is as rewarding an experience as the destination. We thank each other for what has been an enjoyable and edifying excursion of intellectual enquiry and companionship.

We owe a special word of gratitude to Arthur Kroeber, author of Chapter 3. Arthur has analysed the Chinese economy for years as a long-term Beijing resident. He is a good friend, author of *China's Economy: What Everyone Needs to Know*, and managing director of GaveKal Dragonomics.

The remainder of the book is a product of co-authorship. The Introduction and Chapter 6 were written jointly, sentence by sentence. Linda took the lead on Chapters 1 and 2, Bates on Chapters 4 and 5. Both of us have extensively edited, rephrased, and restructured all of the chapters. Our intention has been to speak as one.

Numerous people have helped us along the way, for which we are greatly appreciative. The book project is an integral part of the public policy initiative China Matters Ltd, which Linda founded in early 2015, thanks to key sponsors PwC, Rio Tinto and several federal government departments.

Supporters of both the book project and the initiative include an eclectic group of prominent Australians: China Matters current board directors (in addition to Bates and Linda) Stephen FitzGerald, Liam Forde, Allan Gyngell and Andrew Parker; former board directors Frances Adamson, Andrew Harding and Warwick Smith; advisory council chair Michael Wesley and advisory council members Geremie Barmé, Kerry Brown, Graham Fletcher, Tim Lane, Peter Leahy, David Olsson, Jonathan Pain, Richard Rigby, Laurie Smith, Julian Snelder, Andrew Stoler and Hugh White. Many of these supporters reviewed parts of the manuscript, as did Nick Bisley, Amy King, Ryan Manual, James Reilly and Mark Thirlwell.

Many other individuals who have no formal role in China Matters have been extremely supportive of our work: Richard Maude, Chris Moraitis, Martin Parkinson, Dennis Richardson, Michael Thawley and Peter Varghese. In addition, we thank dozens of public servants and experts in Australia, China and the United States who have been generous with their time and insights as we explored the Australia–China relationship. We express a sincere thank you to all.

The China Matters team has been a terrific source of assistance. We very much appreciate the input of Hannah Bretherton, Michael Chi, Jacinta Keast, Virginia Lee, Oliver Young and Sophia Zou. We are in particular indebted to Jackson Kwok for his research assistance, review work and editorial advice.

Bates would also like to thank David Capie and Rob Ayson of the Centre for Strategic Studies at Victoria University of Wellington, where he spent six weeks as the Kippenberger Visiting Professor conducting research and writing for this book.

We are grateful to our publisher, Black Inc., and especially Chris Feik and Rebecca Bauert, for their enthusiasm for this undertaking as well as their ongoing professional advice. Although we have had tremendous editorial support, we as co-authors naturally take all responsibility for remaining errors.

Finally, our better-halves – Bates' wife Sarah Palmer and Linda's husband Chris Lanzit – deserve our most heartfelt expression of gratitude. Their constant encouragement and inspiration ensured the fulfilment of this book's journey from start to finish.

Sydney, 3 January 2017
Bates Gill and Linda Jakobson

Acronyms and abbreviations

ACRI Australia-China Relations Institute

ADIZ Air defence identification zone

AIIB Asian Infrastructure Investment Bank

ALP Australian Labor Party

ASEAN Association of Southeast Asian Nations

BIT Bilateral investment treaty

CCDI Central Commission for Discipline Inspection

CCTV China Central Television

CDB China Development Bank

CPC Communist Party of China

CRI China Radio International

CSSA Chinese Students and Scholars Association

FDI Foreign direct investment

FIRB Foreign Investment Review Board

FTZ Free Trade Zone

GDP Gross domestic product

HADR Humanitarian assistance and disaster relief

KMT Kuomintang (Chinese Nationalist Party)

LSG Leading small groups

NGO Non-governmental organisation

NSRF New Silk Road Fund

OBOR One Belt, One Road

OECD Organisation for Economic Cooperation and Development

PBOC People's Bank of China

PLA People's Liberation Army

PRC People's Republic of China

SOE State-owned enterprise

THAAD Terminal High Altitude Area Defense

UN United Nations

INTRODUCTION
Why this book?

China matters to Australia.

Australia is affected by nearly every aspect of China's remarkable transformation. There are about 225 million middle-class Chinese households.[1] They dream about seeing the world. Annually Chinese citizens make over 120 million trips overseas; about 1 million of them visited Australia in 2015. They know much more about the world and their own country, including their own government, than they did a mere ten years ago. China has 1.3 billion mobile phone accounts, 720 million internet subscribers, and 700 million and 280 million monthly active users of social media platforms WeChat and Weibo respectively. The growing desire among Chinese people for greater openness poses a challenge for the Communist Party of China (CPC), and raises the possibility of future political instability in a country of tremendous importance to Australia.

Australia is the G20 country most dependent on China in terms of export revenue. Nearly one-third of Australia's exports by value are sold to China. Australian exports to China are worth more than

Australia's exports to the United States, Germany, the United Kingdom, South Korea, France, Canada and all of South-East Asia combined.[2] Australians wanting to visit China are offered direct flights to fifteen Chinese cities, the smallest one being Fuzhou, with 3.2 million residents.[3] Direct flights are set to grow, attracting Australians wishing to experience Chinese cuisine, culture and the fascination of Chinese life.

Among Australians the second most widely spoken language is Mandarin Chinese. Chinese immigrants have been part of Australian society since the early nineteenth century. Today there are 482,000 Australian residents who were born in the People's Republic of China (PRC). About 1 million people living in Australia identify as ethnically Chinese. Over the past four decades 115 sister city and sister state relationships have been formed between Australia and China; the list even includes the partnership between Wagga Wagga, a town of 63,000 inhabitants, and Kunming, a provincial capital with 100 times that population.[4]

China now commands the largest number of naval vessels in Asia, with more than 300 surface ships and seventy submarines.[5] China's ongoing military modernisation transforms the security environment for Australia. Australia's alliance with the United States risks entangling Australia in a US–China conflict. The uncertainties surrounding US President Donald Trump's foreign policies further complicate US–China–Australia relations.

In spite of China's importance, many Australians do not have a nuanced understanding of the reasons for this or fully appreciate the risks and opportunities involved in relations with China. Upon moving to this country several years ago we were both struck by a sense that Australians do not entirely grasp how vast China's impact will be on Australia's future. We were also taken aback by Australia's lack of homegrown China expertise, especially in Chinese politics, foreign affairs and security policy. We were strongly encouraged by a diverse group of prominent Australians to write this book to catalyse a more balanced and realistic public discourse on relations with China. Our interest is to expand awareness, inform public opinion and advance sound policy on the complexities, opportunities and challenges of China's rise.

This book provides a portrait of China today – its aspirations, politics, economics, and projection of influence and power. It then addresses the question of what China today will mean for Australia tomorrow, and how Australia should better prepare for that future. The first five chapters focus on China; the final chapter zeroes in on Australia's ties with China.

This is a daunting task. While Chinese society is vastly more open and multifaceted than even ten years ago, there is much we do not know. The Party remains secretive and resistant to scrutiny. Something as simple as how often the top leadership meets or its meeting agenda is not publicly available information. But decades of living and working in China help us appreciate Chinese perspectives on their society and their place in the world. With sixty years of combined experience analysing Chinese politics, economics and foreign policy, we have been constantly inspired to interpret and understand a changing China.

Why China matters
Understanding the China Dream

Many Australians would have first heard about the China Dream after Xi Jinping took leadership of the Party and the military in

China in late 2012. The China Dream encapsulates Xi's aim to make China wealthy and strong again. Xi has repeatedly said that his prime mission as CPC leader is to oversee the rejuvenation of the Chinese nation so that Chinese people do not suffer the humiliations of past centuries when foreigners invaded and occupied parts of China. Such grand ambition has profound implications for Australia.

In reality, leading thinkers within the Party had begun to discuss a concept called the China Dream in the years before Xi's ascent to power. They were worried about the ideological confusion among CPC members after such rapid economic and social change and sought to identify an easy-to-digest narrative that would appeal to people's hopes and aspirations, not only to their material expectations. Xi grasped the concept and made it his signature slogan.[6] Two aspects of Xi's China Dream are especially noteworthy. In the Party's view, the China Dream can only be achieved under CPC leadership. Second, the China Dream is a vehicle for Xi to reach out to the middle classes, whose support the Party desperately needs as China continues its modernisation drive.

Understanding the China Dream is a useful starting point for Australians and others to comprehend China today because it encompasses many of the contradictions that vex the people of China and their leaders. Chapter 1 delves into these contradictions.

It is important for Australians to grasp just how much the Party's emphasis on China's 'century of humiliation' still colours the way many Chinese people view the outside world. In a similar vein, another contradiction evident in the China Dream states that China seeks to rise peacefully. Yet it insists that China's sovereign rights cannot be violated – and that includes disputed maritime rights – which pits China against some of its neighbours.

Disparities and dissatisfaction

Of course Chinese people have their own dreams, and not all of them are in harmony with the official dream. Most Chinese people above all dream of living in a society devoid of social injustices. But the CPC leadership is unwilling to take the crucial steps to ensure a more equitable and just society – a subject to be explored in more detail in Chapter 2.

Chapter 2 focuses on China's evolving society. It first charts key milestones, starting from the 1980s, which transformed relations between state and citizen. Next it describes many of the unhealthy trends that emerged when the energy of Chinese people was unleashed to pursue wealth and a wider range of personal choices. These trends include the widening gaps between rich and poor, between the inland areas and the coastal provinces, and between the privileged political classes and ordinary people. These disparities cause widespread discontent among hundreds of millions of Chinese. Furthermore, corruption, social injustice and the toll of environmental degradation embitter Chinese citizens regardless of income level and social rank.

The speed with which Xi centralised power in his own hands surprised most observers. He circumvented the government bureaucracy by creating new CPC-led agencies. He ordered CPC members to be honest, scrupulous and hard-working models for their fellow citizens. As one of his first measures Xi initiated an anti-corruption campaign unlike any other during China's reform decades. Thousands of CPC officials and officers of the People's Liberation Army (PLA), including senior leaders, have been punished.

Australian media has stressed the anti-corruption campaign's popularity among ordinary Chinese. While this may be accurate, it does not necessarily mean that Xi is universally popular. As Chapter 2 explains, Xi has also implemented several policies that curb some of the freedoms to which Chinese people had become accustomed; for example, internet usage has been more tightly censored under Xi. Even mildly contrary thinking is more severely dealt with than during his predecessor's ten years in power. This is important for Australians to understand because many of Xi's policies are taking China in a direction that is even further away from the values Australians uphold, such as freedom of speech and media openness. After all, for years many China watchers, political leaders and informed citizens the world over thought that as China grew more prosperous its politics would become more pluralistic and tolerant.

It is also important to recognise that Xi's aversion to political reform stems from a fear of the Party losing control and suffering the fate of the Soviet Communist Party. Thus while he speaks of the need to implement the rule of law and undoubtedly is aware that this would require making the justice system independent of the Communist Party, he dares not take that step. In contemplating this dilemma for Chinese leaders, Chapter 2 concludes with a focus on the future prospects for CPC survival.

Will China's economy continue to grow?

The Chinese economy is a force of great consequence for Australia, the region and indeed the world. The rapid and unprecedented growth seen in the past three decades has not only lifted hundreds of millions of Chinese out of poverty and transformed the country into an economic powerhouse, it has directly contributed to Australia's prosperity.

But the Chinese economy has the potential to break – just as profoundly as it did make – the Australian economy. It all depends on whether the Party can transform China's growth model from capital-intensive to consumption-led growth, and if Australia can respond to that transformation. Chapter 3 assesses China's capacity to achieve this transition from an era of capital mobilisation to one of capital efficiency. It projects two scenarios, one successful and one unsuccessful, which will determine China's economic future and its implications for Australia and the world.

China's recent history has been marked by massive spending on infrastructure to build the fundamentals of a modern, export-led industrial economy: freeways, railways, harbours, airports, power generation systems, telecommunications networks, manufacturing facilities, urban agglomerations, housing, and the like. But this period of booming capital investment or resource mobilisation is coming to an end. Building yet another high-speed train or airport or new urban centre will not contribute as much to China's growth as in the past – and we know China is increasingly facing overcapacity problems: too much heavy industry, too much housing and too much under-utilised capital stock. The challenge for the future will be to rely less on resource mobilisation and capital investment and more on extracting efficiencies from those resources and moving towards a greater consumption-led growth model. The Chinese economy must shift towards the provision of services, fuelled by the ever-increasing wealth of the Chinese consumer. There is evidence that this shift is already underway, with the services sector share of GDP increasing to more than 50 per cent in 2016 and the industrial share decreasing to 41 per cent. However, China's ratio of gross debt to GDP is dangerously high at about 250 per cent.

This is a very difficult transition, fraught with both economic and political risk. Whereas the past growth model could benefit from state-led and state-owned investments and decision-making – and with less concern over efficient uses of capital – China's future growth model will need to get the state out of the way, be more focused on efficiency, and allow the market to have a far larger role in determining the allocation of resources.

While the Party has acknowledged the imperative of allowing the market freer rein, it seems unable to resist the temptation to step in when economic growth seems at risk. Ultimately the Party must withstand a number of unpopular and uncomfortable consequences in order to achieve successful economic reform.

China's image and influence in Australia

Chinese civilisation has always held the power of attraction. Throughout most of its long history, China was able through its culture and material achievements to draw others into its orbit. This early example of China's soft power – that is, the ability to achieve preferred outcomes through persuasion and attraction rather than through coercion – was the very basis of the tributary system, placing the Middle Kingdom at the centre of Asian culture, politics, economics and diplomacy for most of recorded history.

What aspects of that soft power have survived the past two tumultuous centuries for China? How is today's China seeking to present an attractive image of its past and present to shape our thinking in support of Chinese policies now and in the future? In particular, how is the Party projecting its influence in Australia?

Chapter 4 delves into these questions by looking at the positive and negative aspects of Chinese influence and what it means for Australia. China remains a fascinating place for so many reasons. It has achieved remarkable economic success over a short period of time. It has risen to great power status without resort to warfare. Chinese technology has a global footprint thanks to popular Chinese commercial brands such as Alibaba, Haier, Huawei and Lenovo, and the expansive reach of Chinese social media platforms such as Weibo and WeChat. With a growing diaspora of PRC-born individuals around the world, the presence of PRC norms, values and ideas is likewise on the rise.

Since its founding, the Party has taken the projection of a positive image very seriously, both at home and abroad. This has been the job of the Party's Propaganda Department for nearly 100 years. It is no different today, but the resources and technologies available to China's Party-State are vastly superior to anything the CPC has wielded before to project influence overseas.

As a result, the PRC has in place an extensive network – through traditional and new media, through the growing presence of Chinese overseas, and through its diplomatic missions – to try to present a persuasive and positive image of China, its leaders and their policies.

But several problems lie at the heart of this soft power push. PRC government-directed efforts to influence thinking overseas are ultimately made on behalf of the Party and are aimed at strengthening the legitimacy of its one-party rule both at home and abroad. When the PRC's propaganda efforts demand the loyalty of Australian citizens of Chinese descent or try to persuade Australian politicians to see things Beijing's way, it impinges on the foundation of Australia's democracy. The Party's attempts to portray a positive image of its objectives often run contrary to Australian values and interests.

Nevertheless, Beijing will continue to refine its soft power efforts as one of many instruments to pursue its national goals. Australians must avoid stirring a populist Sino-phobic backlash while also encouraging a more open discussion about the role of PRC government influence in Australia.

Wielding its economic and military power

By their nature, soft power efforts to persuade and attract are often subtle and less visible. Hard power, on the other hand – which aims to achieve a certain goal through coercion and threats – is deliberately overt and confronting. With its growing economic heft and military muscle, China today is in its most powerful position in over 200 years to influence others through hard power means.

Hard power is most often associated with the threat and use of military force. But Australians should also recognise that China's leaders are not shy about exercising economic hard power to threaten and punish other countries to accept their bidding on sensitive issues. Indeed, given the importance of trade with China for their country's prosperity, Australians should be more concerned in the near term about the possibility of Chinese economic coercion – disrupting Australian exports and other business activities with China – than with traditional military threats.

In assessing these points, Chapter 5 details the ascendance of China's economic and military power over the past two decades. By some measures, the PRC is already the world's largest economy. Through the deployment of its immense capital reserves for overseas investment, foreign infrastructure development and development assistance, China's economic clout continues to grow, and so too does the ability to use this clout coercively if and when PRC leaders choose to do so. China's military might has advanced rapidly as a result of double-digit military budget increases every year for most of the past twenty-five years.

The chapter goes on to show how China has been increasingly willing and able to use hard power. To show their displeasure with policies by other countries deemed offensive by China – for example, allowing a visit of the Dalai Lama, tolerating anti-China protests in the name of free speech, or pushing back against China's maritime claims – Chinese leaders have imposed trade restrictions, made business dealings more difficult, and encouraged boycotts by Chinese consumers against the countries in question.

Some twenty years ago, when China's military power was considerably weaker than today, China fired missiles in the waters around Taiwan in an effort to influence the island's democratic elections. The PRC's steady military build-up in the South China Sea since the late 2000s is aimed at intimidating rival claimants into accepting China's territorial claims. These are just two examples of China's growing willingness to use hard power.

Though there are real limits to how China can wield threats and coercion, Australia will not be immune. It seems highly unlikely that Beijing would overtly threaten Australia militarily. But the PRC's military assertiveness in the South and East China seas could draw Australia into a more confrontational situation with China, all the more so if US–China tensions escalate, given that Australia is a treaty ally of the United States. Similarly, tensions over Taiwan's future have re-emerged because Donald Trump has questioned

China's insistence that Taiwan is a part of China. The Trump presidency raises many new questions about the future of US–China relations and their consequences for Australia.

In the near term, military conflict is less likely than the threat or imposition of economic punishments on Australia because of decisions in Canberra that China finds offensive. Chinese state-run media outlets have strongly hinted that such actions would be necessary should Australia go too far in opposing PRC actions in the South China Sea. As much as Australians may wish to avoid it, they need to be better prepared to deal with China's growing hard power capabilities. Drawing from the words of a senior Australian security official, there will inevitably be times when Australia will need to stand up for the values it believes in and bear the brunt of China's wrath.

What should Australia do?

This picture of China is a reminder of just how multi-layered, vibrant, complex and messy Chinese society and the ambitions of its people and leaders have become. This presents Australians with optimistic prospects as well as worrisome possibilities. On the one hand, the dynamism of China today and the rise of the middle classes with their diverse opinions give hope that China will move towards a more just society and a more accountable system of governance. On the other hand, Xi's leadership has cast a shadow over such expectations.

Australia has benefited enormously from China's economic miracle. But it is unclear how willing China's leaders are to implement the dramatic changes required to transform the Chinese economy. This brings uncertainty to Australia's own economic future.

Chinese culture is understandably admired in Australia and around the world. Achievements of contemporary China also evoke appreciation and respect. These include lifting hundreds of millions out of poverty, stemming disease, providing basic education for nearly all and becoming a greater contributor to United Nations peacekeeping and to international efforts to curb illicit trafficking in drugs and people. For over two decades China has been the principal engine of growth for the global economy. Yet China's increased strength raises many concerns about how China will use its power.

These dilemmas loom large for Australia. To address them, Chapter 6 identifies three fundamental Australian interests to assess the pros and cons of deepening relations with China: principles, prosperity and security. For each, we put forward practical recommendations for Australians to consider as they look to take greatest advantage of engagement with China, while minimising the downsides of the relationship.

Lastly, we call on Australian leaders and citizens to think big. Getting China right will advance Australia's future in these unpredictable and transformative times.

1

THE CHINA DREAM
Return of the Middle Kingdom

Dreaming of a better tomorrow

No one living in China during the mid-1980s could have dreamt the China of today. Most city folk dreamt of a slightly bigger apartment so that three generations would not have to share a one- or two-room home. Some also entertained the wish that their child, upon finishing school, would be assigned to a not-too-distant 'work unit', the Chinese term used for a state employer. Others fantasised about being sent abroad by their work unit, and in their wildest imaginings this once-in-a-lifetime trip would be to the United States. Whatever dreams a city resident had were dependent on decisions taken by Chinese government officials. Thirty years ago the Chinese state controlled most aspects of a person's life, starting from where one resided and where one worked. You could not marry, have a child or even buy a train ticket without your superior's written approval – an unbearable existence for anyone who did not get on with their boss.

Back in the mid-1980s ordinary people in the countryside could not imagine being allowed to settle in a city. Many if not most of them dreamt of the day when food would be plentiful and they could save enough money to build a solid house and pass their old age without too much hardship.

Thirty or so years ago any Chinese citizen dismissed the thought of owning a car – let alone a home, or holidaying overseas with the family – as fantasy; not to speak of the diversity of lifestyle choices, job opportunities, dazzling high-rise malls, consumer goods and leisure activities that so many urban Chinese today take for granted.

So when China's current leader, Xi Jinping, in 2012 started promoting his signature China Dream slogan, some middle-aged Chinese who had grown up during the politically turbulent 1960s declared on internet chat sites: 'We are already living the China Dream!'

The China Dream encapsulates an array of Xi's ambitions. He wants to make China modern and successful. He wants to restore the ideological legitimacy and attractiveness of the Party, and he wants to boost the self-confidence of all Chinese, but especially CPC members. Grasping some of the motivations and undercurrents of Xi's China Dream, as well as the dreams of ordinary Chinese, is vital for understanding China today.

Another important dimension is recognising the energy and determination with which hundreds of millions of Chinese have gone about fulfilling their own personal dreams. Since Deng Xiaoping, the architect of the People's Republic's second revolution, set the nation on a path of reform and opening in the late 1970s, people have taken advantage of the freedom of choice brought about by Deng's actions in every conceivable way. Today they may start a company, change jobs, own an apartment (or several), buy airline tickets, educate their child at a private school or even overseas, find a partner using online dating services, and purchase food, consumer goods and just about any other service online. In 1978 the average annual per capita income was US$155; in 2016 it was US$8200.[1]

The relentless desire to make tomorrow a better day still propels China forward. Evan Osnos, an award-winning American journalist who wrote about the years he lived in China (2005–2013), aptly titled his book *Age of Ambition*. He describes a shift in thinking among Chinese people from determinism to a fervent belief in the ability to alter one's life, regardless of the circumstances. As one of the book's characters notes: 'Why should I be like everyone else, just because I was born to a poor family?'[2]

A high degree of ambition certainly is a characteristic Xi shares with Chinese people. But before comparing and contrasting the dreams of China's leaders with those of its populace, it is useful to try to understand what Xi wants to achieve with his China Dream.

While the China Dream alludes to a range of aspirations, it also has some clearly defined objectives. These are the Two Centenary Goals: to 'comprehensively build a moderately prosperous society', defined as doubling 2010 GDP and per capita income by 2021; and to 'build a modern socialist country that is prosperous, strong, democratic, culturally advanced and harmonious' by 2049. In 2021 the Party celebrates its hundredth birthday; 2049 marks a century since the establishment of the People's Republic of China.

Raising the living standards of the Chinese people continues to be the primary focus of the Party under Xi. It is imperative for keeping stability in society and maintaining acceptance of CPC rule. Doubling the 2010 per capita income translates into an average annual income in China of US$9000 by 2021. In purchasing-power terms, that would put China at the same level as Mexico and Brazil.[3] But because China is set to pass the goal of US$9000 before 2021, analysts predict China will by then be on par with Italy.[4]

However, because of the gigantic absolute numbers and mind-boggling disparities of everything related to China, comparisons with other countries rarely capture the whole picture. Per capita income in China is brought down by the 151 million Chinese who still live in extreme poverty (under US$1.90 per day), as well as the 360 million who live on less than US$3.10 per day.[5] Only one-fifth of the population is regarded as wealthy or middle class, loosely defined as a person with a post-secondary education who owns a house and has sufficient disposable income for non-essential consumption and travel. But in absolute numbers that is 225 million households.[6] McKinsey and Co estimates that by 2022, some 300 million urban households will be considered affluent, upper middle class or middle class.[7]

The goal of making China a middle-class society is based on Xi's stated objective to make the private sector 'the decisive factor' in the Chinese economy.[8] As will become evident in the following chapters, this is indeed an ambitious objective.

Xi appeals to cultural greatness

A major aim of Xi's China Dream is to realise the great rejuvenation of the Chinese nation. Just hours after becoming CPC General Secretary in November 2012, Xi said that the Party had 'rallied and led the Chinese people in transforming the poor and backward Old China into an increasingly prosperous and powerful New China, thus opening a completely new horizon for the great renewal of the

Chinese nation'.[9] Two weeks later he led the country's most powerful leaders through an exhibition called 'The Road to Renewal' at the National Museum of China and spoke specifically about the China Dream.

Xi sent a host of messages on that first day as China's new leader. At a nationally televised meeting with the media he spoke unambiguous standard Mandarin, conspicuously avoiding often-incomprehensible Marxist political jargon. That in itself was noteworthy. Xi said he understood that ordinary people aspired to good jobs, better social security, better education for their kids and a better environment. He spoke of China being a great nation with a great people; of China's 5000-year history and its great culture; and of the unusual hardship Chinese people had suffered in the past. He acknowledged the need to resolve the problems of corruption, alienation of CPC officials from the people, and bureaucratism.

There was no mistaking his message. China's new leader wanted to be perceived as a man who has ordinary citizens' interests at heart; who wishes all Chinese to feel pride about belonging to a great nation with a great culture; and who wants China to become strong and respected in the family of nations. In subsequent speeches and writings attributed to Xi, he has emphasised that the China Dream and the rejuvenation of the great Chinese nation entail making China strong again in every conceivable way – economically, militarily, politically, culturally, scientifically, technologically – to make sure the Chinese people do not suffer the humiliations of the past.

Do these desires resonate with Chinese people? Absolutely. The China Dream reflects a historical yearning for wealth, power, respect and global standing. The China Dream fulfils a need to make up for lost time.

Chinese people are no different from any other people in their feelings of pride for their country. Chinese are especially proud of their 5000 years of civilisation, proud of the country's name 'Middle Kingdom', reflecting the perception of China at the centre of the universe, and proud of the nation's immense accomplishments over the past four decades of modernisation. Chinese wish for China to once again be a respected nation in the international community. For most Chinese that means China must be strong. The vast majority of Chinese agree with Xi's vision – and that of the leaders before him – that China must strive to attain wealth, power and greatness.

Xi strikes a chord when he constantly speaks about China's rich cultural heritage. Overseas Chinese, including Australian-Chinese, are proud of that heritage too. This can cause conflicting emotions in those who do not feel an attachment to the PRC or in those who abhor some of the policies of the PRC but still love their Chinese cultural heritage.

Intermingled with understandable pride and patriotism is a legacy of victimhood. Every PRC citizen under the age of seventy was taught – and taught again – at school that Chinese people suffered horribly at the hands of outsiders – especially Japan and Western powers – during the 'century of humiliation', approximately from the 1840s to the 1940s, which indeed they did. They are taught that, had it not been for the Party, the Chinese people would not have 'stood up' in 1949 and hundreds of millions of people would not have been lifted out of poverty and hundreds of millions more would not have moved into the ranks of the middle class. This too is a reasonable statement, though it is first and foremost the Chinese people who deserve credit for these achievements. The 'celebration of national insecurity', as William Callahan of the London School of

Economics has called the ongoing emphasis on national humiliation, is a prominent feature of children's education.[10]

But, importantly, the narrative continues through adulthood. New books, articles, television programs, theatre, operas, theme parks and museum exhibitions today still send subtle or less subtle messages about the need to be vigilant so that the century of humiliation is never repeated. To quote Zheng Wang of Seton Hall University, the century of humiliation is a 'lasting trauma seared into the national conscious [sic]'.[11] One is constantly reminded that China was subjugated by outsiders because it was weak, and the Party is to be thanked for making China strong again.

Humiliation can also be a driver of energy, according to China scholars Orville Schell and John Delury. In their book *Wealth and Power: China's Long March to the Twenty-first Century*, they write: 'Through a strange alchemy, based on an old Confucian idea that humiliation stimulates effort, the shame that stemmed from humiliation and defeat generated a steely determination to become strong again.'[12]

Whether a stimulant or a depressant, the elaborate layers of humiliation and shame that are part of the national psyche in China today create troubling undercurrents. Humiliation and shame inhibit the formation of a neutral view of other countries. During any one day, a Chinese person listening to the radio might hear a senior official point out that China seeks peaceful relations with other countries, based on mutual trust and mutual respect – and China expects others to adhere to this principle as well. From another official the listener will hear a reference to the century of humiliation, implicitly warning that foreigners can never be trusted because they might push China down again. Some officials go so far as to say that is precisely what the United States, Japan, and other Westerners are generally trying to do.

The ongoing public education that keeps alive the lessons of the century of humiliation is not unique to Xi's leadership. With each new CPC general secretary, the messaging has become more sophisticated to appeal to new generations of Chinese in a connected and globalised world.

The explicit goal of the 'rejuvenation of the Chinese nation' is not novel to Xi Jinping either. Sun Yat-sen (1866–1925), considered by people on both the mainland and Taiwan as the father of modern China, spoke of the need for rejuvenation. So did twenty-first-century reform leaders Jiang Zemin and Hu Jintao.

Even use of the word 'dream' was not coined by Xi. Chinese writers had incorporated the word into various arguments over the past decade during fierce internal debates about how to make China strong and wealthy. New terms were adopted in the 1990s to replace old Marxist-Leninist maxims which became less important as a justification for CPC policies. This was especially so after the crumbling of the Berlin Wall and the collapse of the Soviet Union. Chinese leaders relied less on ideology and more on national pride. This changed in the months following Xi's ascent to power. Xi is intent on reinvigorating the Party. He has tried hard to reinforce the importance of ideology alongside national pride.

Xi's appeal to ideology is likely to be an uphill battle. It is not at all certain that CPC members, let alone ordinary Chinese citizens, are ready to return to the days when policies were justified by ideological reasoning. The appeal to patriotism is complex too because the CPC equates love for one's country with love for the Party. Whether Chinese people actually embrace this notion is also questionable.

The Party intentionally stokes nationalist sentiment to reinforce the message of the Party's indispensability. As Xi Jinping has made clear, the goals of rejuvenating the nation, keeping China unified and avoiding anything akin to the century of humiliation must (and can only) happen under the leadership of the Party.

The era of submissiveness is over

Xi's rise to power and promotion of the China Dream have been accompanied by a ferocious expression of nationalist views in officially sanctioned media outlets. At the turn of the twenty-first century, hardcore nationalists who were anti-Western were still considered relatively marginalised and were only allowed to rant and rage online. Today they are mainstream voices in the public sphere.

There are numerous reasons for this, including competition among television, radio, online and print media outlets as a consequence of the rise of social media, and, unmistakably, the merging of top-down state nationalism and bottom-up popular nationalism under the metaphorical umbrella of Xi's China Dream. Here state nationalism means the interests of the Communist state to ensure loyalty of the citizenry. The leadership uses nationalism to bolster the population's faith in the Party's ability to guide the nation through an era of rapid and turbulent transformation.[13] Popular nationalism is expressed in emotional outbursts at perceived slights to China and the Chinese people.

What has further changed since Xi's ascent to power in late 2012 is his emphasis on the need for China – while upholding stability – to forcefully defend its rights and interests when dealing with outsiders. During his predecessor's ten years in power, maintaining stability was the overriding objective. 'Upholding stability' was code for avoiding risks, especially in the international arena, to ensure domestic political stability and economic growth. China needed to continue to modernise and accumulate power. Of slightly lesser importance was defending sovereignty and territorial integrity. Under Xi these two goals appear in official texts in reverse order: first comes defending sovereignty and territorial integrity, next comes stability.

In practice, this means that in the seas off China, for example, safeguarding sovereign rights is promoted over maintaining stability. When previously China Coast Guard vessels were ordered to withdraw from any stand-off in disputed waters, now they are allowed to 'act more resolutely' against what China perceives as intruders in China's sovereign waters.[14] In security policy parlance, it means Xi is more willing than his predecessors to allow China's security forces to take risks to send a signal to the region and to the United States that China will defend what it perceives as its own.

From the perspective of many Chinese people, Chinese officials had to be submissive in their dealings with the international community for the sake of China's modernisation during the first three decades of reform. This was particularly relevant to interactions with the United States and other industrialised countries. According to this thinking, outsiders dictated the terms of China's engagement with the world because China was poor, weak and isolated. China needed the outside world more than the outside world needed China. Today, China still needs the outside world, but this is played down in the official narrative. China sees itself as richer, stronger and more experienced internationally and with Xi's endorsement it should indeed be more assertive in defending its rights.

'Rights protection' is all the rage in China today. It is useful to numerous interest groups upon which the Party relies to maintain political stability in an increasingly multifaceted society. Many of these actors ardently support China's display of its wealth and power. They stand to gain, for example, from China's expansion and defence of its maritime interests, whether commercially, or through increased government funding, or in terms of prestige. These actors comprise various parts of local governments, law enforcement agencies and the People's Liberation Army (PLA), as well as industries ranging from fisheries to energy and resources companies, shipbuilding and tourism. They grasp every opportunity to persuade the government to approve new fishing bases, rescue centres, tourist attractions, larger and better-equipped patrol vessels, resource exploration and legal instruments to codify claims. In the present nationalistic political atmosphere, it is nearly impossible to denounce an action taken in the name of protecting China's rights.

Of course scores of competing objectives counterbalance nationalist demands for a forceful defence of China's rights. There are numerous actors – agencies of local governments and business and industry groups such as tourism and consumer goods exporters – which stand to benefit from more joint ventures and greater trade with neighbouring countries. In general they desire more congenial ties with the region. They in turn make use of the slogan China Dream. Their objectives serve to temper nationalist inclinations. In any country, policymaking and policy implementation require balancing diverse interests. China is no exception.

Xi's mammoth One Belt, One Road (OBOR) initiative has the potential to create new and powerful interest groups which could redirect attention and resources away from the contentious South

China Sea disputes. Though still in its infancy, OBOR envisions connecting China with more than sixty countries through land and sea routes via the ancient Silk Road stretching from China through Central Asia to Europe and via a newly imagined Maritime Silk Road from China through South-East Asia to Africa and Europe. The strategy focuses on five areas: infrastructure, trade, policy, finance and people. It is too early to tell whether this ambitious plan will remain a lofty goal or become the driving force for China's strategic engagement with the world. Even if only half of this initiative comes to fruition over the next three or four decades, it would speed up China's transition to becoming the dominant regional power – in other words, realising an unspoken part of Xi's China Dream.

America looms large

In spite of China's growing confidence, many Chinese argue that China continues to kowtow to the West, particularly the United States, allowing Westerners to dictate the agenda of engagement. America looms large when Chinese, especially middle-class and wealthy city dwellers, think about China in a global context. The oldest thriving civilisation has in less than forty years broken every imaginable record of development in history, and is today in the minds of Chinese citizens either on the verge of becoming or already is a great power. The comparison with the United States, the world's most powerful nation, is incessant.

The global financial crisis transformed the Chinese view of the United States and marked a turning point in bilateral relations. Chinese people, from ordinary citizens to the senior echelons of officialdom, were shocked by the collapse of Lehman Brothers and the ensuing financial chaos. Chinese were incredulous that a powerful economy like that of the United States could be so vulnerable. The repeated praise of China as a reliable and stable economic force by countries across the globe resulted in a spate of articles describing the United States as a country in decline and assessing China's international standing in a new light. From about 2009 onward, following the success of the Beijing Olympics in 2008, Chinese officials and scholars started to seriously contemplate how to convert China's economic power into political and cultural influence around the world.

After Barack Obama took office in 2009, it became clear that the United States would aim to increase its diplomatic, military and economic resources in the Asia-Pacific, a strategy which in 2011 became known as the 'pivot'. This was viewed by many Chinese analysts as a policy to keep China from rising and ensure the primacy of American power in the Asia-Pacific. Hence, the global financial crisis and the US pivot to Asia only strengthened the aspiration inherent in Xi's China Dream to be treated as an equal by the United States. Another part of the China Dream, which Xi has not elaborated on in public, is the aspiration of China to become the dominant power in the Asia-Pacific. But Xi alluded to this in 2014 when he said that Asians should take responsibility for Asian security.

The two-way love-hate relationship between the United States and China over the past 200 years is well documented. Throughout the 1980s and most of the 1990s it was common to hear Chinese speak of the United States as heaven on earth. Most Chinese parents still dream of their child studying at an American university; many young people aspire to that dream too. In December 1978, fifty-two Chinese students arrived to study in the United States, sent off with the approval of Deng Xiaoping. Today, more than 300,000 Chinese students are enrolled in schools in the United States. Yet many of these same students and their parents resent the manner in which American political leaders treat China. They often perceive American leaders as condescending and disdainful of China's new global standing.

Chinese wish for respect, regardless of the degree of their enthusiasm for the United States or their suspicion of Washington's intentions. One wonders whether any display of respect will ultimately be sufficient to placate the resentment whipped up by the Communist Party leadership's constant reminders of the century of humiliation. Thoughtful intellectuals concede in private that this focus on victimhood spurs unhealthy nationalist sentiments. They say that a more nuanced interpretation of Chinese history is not part of Xi's China Dream.

Many kinds of dreams

When asked, 'What does the China Dream mean?', some Chinese people will laugh. Sometimes they laugh to hide their awkwardness or embarrassment. It might not have occurred to them to think more deeply about a slogan handed down by the Party. Chinese people have been exposed to CPC slogans from birth, so in many cases a new one merely numbs the mind. Sometimes the laugh expresses amusement: poking fun at political slogans, especially with the help of puns, is a national pastime. Those who laugh are not necessarily opposed to Xi's desire for China to attain wealth and respect. Rather, the cynicism they feel towards the Party is so great that a serious inquiry about one of its slogans is either odd or funny.

Sometimes the laugh is more of a snort. Some Chinese say the China Dream is hollow. One such person, a university lecturer, opined that at least Harmonious Society, a key slogan of Xi's prede-cessor, Hu Jintao, reflected the challenge of mitigating growing contradictions within society as China became more pluralistic and some people accumulated wealth faster than others. This academic said he felt insulted when he first heard Xi speak about the China Dream because it has no intellectual substance.

Whatever Chinese people think – or do not think – about the China Dream, they are constantly reminded that, for the China Dream to be fulfilled, all the nation's resources will need to be har-nessed. The slogan pops up in newspaper articles, radio and television programs, internet chat sites, billboards and official speeches. School children compete to provide the most innovative interpretation of realising the China Dream. Recruitment ads for the PLA encourage young adults to be a part of achieving the China Dream. Local officials across the country write proposals to their superiors stating that in order to fulfil the China Dream sufficient funds need to be allocated to this or that project.

People naturally have their own dreams. It is common to hear the China Dream playfully described by middle-class urbanites, nouveau riche holiday-seekers and widely travelled academics as a visa-free world for PRC citizens. Joking aside, they speak of the enormous change in their lives since the Party loosened controls on acquiring a passport. Today it is the visa regulations of other coun-tries that inhibit Chinese travel enthusiasm. About 120 million Chinese travelled abroad in 2015, more than twenty times the num-ber of Chinese travellers in 1995.[15] Middle-class urban Chinese often remark favourably on the quality of life in industrialised coun-tries, which, regardless of how much richer China becomes, they will only ever enjoy when they are outside China.

According to a survey conducted in China in mid-2015 by the Pew Research Center of the United States, Chinese aspire to live in a less corrupt and more just society in a less polluted and safer environment in which one can find a job, provide good education for one's offspring, and trust that food is safe.[16] This survey, alongside many others conducted by Chinese researchers, confirms the citizenry's perceptions of Chinese leadership's greatest challenges: the slowing of economic growth, severe environmental degradation, patchy food security, rampant corruption, poor health care, income inequality and uneven educational opportunities.

Corruption has become a code word for many ills, some of which will be the focus of the next chapter. It is politically correct in China to oppose corruption, hence the inclusion of corruption in contemporary surveys done by Chinese academics. Chinese leaders since Deng Xiaoping have acknowledged that corruption is the cancer that threatens to kill the Party. Each top leader has overseen an anti-corruption campaign. Before Xi, however, ordinary citizens merely shrugged off such campaigns, sometimes quoting an old Chinese proverb about 'killing the chicken to scare the monkeys'. In the past, a corrupt deputy mayor may have been made a scapegoat and been imprisoned or even executed, yet corrupt practices would soon flourish again.

Xi's all-out effort to eliminate corruption is described in media reports as a key reason for his popularity among ordinary folk. However, in private conversations urban Chinese speak bitterly not only about the effects of corruption in their lives, but also about social injustice more broadly. And they very pointedly talk about the effects of nepotism and arbitrary decisions meted out by police, village leaders, the courts and higher officials. Though 'a society governed by the rule of law' is not terminology commonly heard in conversation with ordinary people in China, they do say – when pressed about their 'personal China Dream' – that they wish their children would live to see a more just society, one in which all citizens are treated equally under the law. Thus far, this is not what Xi Jinping's China Dream has delivered. In this respect the dreams of Chinese citizens are in contradiction with today's reality.

Chinese people, generally speaking, are first and foremost keen to get on with their lives. Though Xi has mentioned the importance of the dreams and efforts of each individual, the China Dream calls upon Chinese citizens to make personal sacrifices in order to better the nation. The China Dream is very much a collective project led by the Party, and certainly differs in its emphasis from the American Dream. As Chinese scholar Yu Jianrong summarised: 'The American Dream refers to the dream of the protection of individual rights. The Chinese Dream is the dream of strengthening the country's rights.'[17]

Here lies a great paradox, one of many in a country racing towards modernity under the leadership of a Party that wants to assert control over people's minds. Chinese people do, in an aspirational sense, share Xi's dream of rejuvenating the Chinese nation. But few are volunteering to put their personal goals on hold for the sake of the country – or the Party.

2.

SOCIAL CHANGE
Will the political fabric unravel?

From 1989 to today: astonishing changes

The freedom for individuals to determine many aspects of their personal lives is the most astonishing change in China since the late 1970s. Reflecting on the transformation of Chinese society, the most remarkable development is not the mind-boggling rise in purchasing power or the number of new shopping malls and residential villa compounds which have transformed the cities of China, but rather the increase in personal freedom. Chinese people under the age of forty – that is, about 750 million people – have no experience of a time when every decision affecting one's life, including the job one had or when the family's one and only child was to be conceived, was determined by the government.

In 1989, when Western media transmitted images of Chinese student demonstrators converging on Tiananmen Square in Beijing to 'demand democracy', readers and viewers were rarely – if ever – told that one of the students' key demands was the right for college graduates to be granted a say in the work unit they were assigned to upon graduation. It was common for college graduates to be sent far away from home and family, in the name of fulfilling one's duty to participate in the modernisation of the motherland. A university degree holder was an extremely privileged member of society. It was a given that the state, having provided a university education, had the right to decide where a person's skills would be best utilised. Thus, if a work unit in Xi'an needed someone with your educational background, you moved to Xi'an, even if your parents lived in Tianjin, some 900 kilometres away, and your university sweetheart and soon-to-be-spouse and his whole family were Shanghainese, another 900 kilometres or so from Tianjin in another direction. The future was bleak. Transferring from one work unit to another was either impossible or extremely difficult, and sometimes required political connections and more often than not bribes to the administrators in charge of personnel issues.

Although the Chinese government violently crushed the 1989 movement, it eventually acquiesced to this particular demand. From the early 1990s onward, a graduating university student's preferences were officially considered in the state's job allocation. Another transformative factor was the fundamental shift in the entire job market. In 1992, after Deng Xiaoping encouraged his compatriots to reform the economy even faster, government officials started to 'jump into the sea'. This term was used to describe government officials who left their work unit to become entrepreneurs. Many university graduates also opted to reject the offer from a work unit and instead started their own businesses, or independently found employment in either the state or private sector. This loosening of controls on employment, which occurred roughly during the first half of the 1990s, was revolutionary. It was as life-changing to the relations between citizens and the state as the decision over a decade earlier to allow communes to disband and permit farmers to sell a portion of their crops on the free market.

A popular saying among urban Chinese in the 1990s captured the mood: 'If you don't bother the government, the government won't bother you.' This reflected the shift in China towards a tacit acknowledgement of the importance of an individual's right to make personal choices, and away from the overarching focus on a person's obligations towards the state, which in the PRC meant and continues to mean obligations towards the Communist Party of China (CPC). A new social class emerged, composed of urban adults in their twenties, thirties and forties – mostly small-scale entrepreneurs and service providers but also artists, filmmakers, musicians, writers and designers. These people had no dealings with the state. They rented a home or an office on the free market, shopped for groceries on the free market, and earned a living relying on their own wits. As long as they did not publicly challenge the rule of the Party, no government or CPC official meddled in their activities. It was a type of freedom envied by anyone who remained in a state work unit. It took another decade – until 2003 – before a work-unit employee gained even the right to marry without their employer's permission.

The one personal freedom that the state continued to assert control over was reproductive rights. The one-child policy, which was introduced in the late 1970s, was formally phased out in 2015. Over the years, especially as of the late 1990s, many exemptions were granted under the strict policy. For example, by the mid-2000s most rural families were allowed to have a second child if the first child was a girl. In the cities middle-class and wealthy families, especially those who did not work for the state, opted to pay the hefty fine imposed for a second child if they wanted more offspring.

Today in China, with just over 8 per cent of the Chinese working population in state jobs, the vast majority of Chinese do not rely on the state for a living.[1] In any city large or small there are wealthy, upper-middle-class and middle-class families who, like the unattached citizens of the 1990s, have few if any dealings with officialdom.

The key groups who today are still subordinate to government scrutiny of their personal lives are public servants throughout the country, employees of state-owned enterprises (SOEs) or work units such as universities, state theatre companies, state hospitals and so on, and residents of rural villages. The divide between urban areas and the countryside is still stark. The previously rigid household registration system identifying persons as either urban or rural residents and thus determining their access to education and health care, for example, is being reformed. But tens of millions living in villages are still at the mercy of their local CPC officials for many issues directly affecting their everyday lives.

In part, the loosening of controls over employment and the movement of workers within the country was fundamental to economic reform and maintaining faster economic growth, as Deng had urged. It was also critical to restoring social stability after the 1989 people's movement, which grew spontaneously out of the initial Tiananmen student protests and made even greater and more far-reaching demands on the Party. Chinese leaders were shocked when a million Beijing residents and millions more in over a hundred cities across China took advantage of the senior leadership's indecisiveness over how to deal with the student demonstrations by taking to the streets themselves to protest against inflation and to

35

oppose corruption and nepotism. In the months following the bru-
tal crackdown of 4 June 1989, CPC conservatives regained the upper
hand. The need to adhere to ideological correctness, including
pledging allegiance to the Party, was emphasised at every turn.
Those who wanted China to modernise rapidly were criticised when
they tried to warn of the consequences of a slowing economy in
internal meetings.

Once Deng made it clear during his Southern Tour in early 1992
that he favoured rapid economic reform, an implicit social pact
formed gradually between the rulers and the ruled. The Party
adhered to policies that ensured rapid economic growth, facilitating
the expansion of a nascent middle class. The citizenry went all out
to take advantage of the economic opportunities. The Party survived
intact. CPC leaders were convinced that they should never again
allow dissatisfaction to be voiced by protesters on the street. Nor
should they permit debates about the future direction of China's
political system. Ideology was not ignored but certainly demoted to
a secondary status. If you didn't bother the government, the government didn't bother you.

Xi Jinping's challenges

By the early 2010s, as Xi Jinping prepared to assume leadership, the
loosened restrictions on employment and personal freedoms had
begun to have troubling consequences for China's continued modernisation and social stability. One was urbanisation. Roughly 500
million people moved from rural areas to the cities during the reform
era.[2] This migration spurred the largest process of urbanisation in
history. It also created immense social problems, and, along with

rapid industrialisation, has had a dramatic impact on the environment. The air quality in most Chinese cities is unhealthy in the extreme. According to a 2015 study cited by a Tsinghua University scholar, air pollution accounts for up to 1.6 million deaths per year in China; this is the equivalent of about 4000 deaths per day and 17 per cent of all deaths in China.[3] The groundwater in over half of China's cities is classified as 'poor' or 'very poor'.[4]

A second consequence was the emergence of severe disparities in living standards and social status. These include the gaps between rich and poor (including a widening gap between urban and rural incomes), between coastal areas and inland provinces, as well as the rift between privileged political classes and common folk. In less than thirty-five years of reform and opening, China had become a polarised nation in terms of income, access to services, and social standing. A nationwide survey conducted by Chinese researchers in 2014 suggested that mobility among the low- and lower-middle classes had stagnated, and people from those groups had little confidence that they could improve their situation.[5] Xi took leadership of a country with not only serious economic challenges but also a populace disillusioned with and in some quarters dissatisfied with the CPC leadership. As a result, greater numbers of wealthy and even middle-class Chinese will emigrate.

Some of these disparities are traditional: over the centuries the overwhelming majority of Chinese were poor and only a tiny minority had wealth and privilege. But during the first three decades of the PRC, equality was promoted as a lofty aspiration. Elderly Chinese still reminisce about the Mao Zedong years, when everyone was equally poor. The term 'everyone' is an exaggeration, as even during the Mao era some Communist cadres had privileges, but what is important is the widespread nostalgia about the ideal of equality. In 2015 a rural household earned on average about 10,500 RMB per year (approximately A$2050), while the national urban household average was 2.75 times higher. These figures portray just a part of the picture. By every measure, the quality of life in a city is higher than in the countryside because access to health care, social welfare and education are all far superior than that in rural areas. An urban child is seven times more likely to be accepted into university than a child raised in the countryside.[6]

China now has some 1.33 million millionaires.[7] Depending on how you calculate poverty, some 151 million people still want for basic necessities.[8]

China's Gini coefficient, a measure of inequality based on income distribution, has grown sharply over the past three decades. In 1981, China's Gini coefficient was 0.29.[9] In 2015, it was 0.46.[10] A coefficient above 0.40 is considered by the World Bank to represent extreme inequality. In other top economies – the United States, Germany, Japan and Australia – the Gini coefficients in 2015 were 0.41, 0.30, 0.32 and 0.34 respectively.[11]

In sum, although per capita income has grown in China and the number of people living in dire poverty has plummeted, income inequality has skyrocketed. This gives rise to social tensions that did not exist before. Low-income families in urban areas resent their place at the bottom of the social ladder. In some cases they are even less well-off or have fewer opportunities than some rural residents who have become successful as entrepreneurs. Many low-income urban families are headed by blue-collar workers who had a stable income and guaranteed social benefits – health insurance and old-age pensions – in an age when state-owned enterprises provided jobs for life and full benefits. The guarantees disappeared when state-owned enterprises were expected to be profitable and started to lay off employees.

Geographical differences in incomes are considerable too. A Shanghai resident earns four times more than an urban resident in the inland province of Gansu, China's poorest province.[12] This gap is even wider than in Brazil. Xi has stressed that no region can be left behind, but he faces an uphill battle. Raw materials churned out by many Chinese inland provinces to satisfy the global commodity boom are no longer in such great demand. The GDP of the inland province of Shaanxi is 1.2 trillion RMB, compared to 3.7 trillion RMB in eastern Jiangsu, China's second-wealthiest province. Economic growth is churning along at 8.5 per cent in Jiangsu while only at 2.8 per cent in Shaanxi.[13]

Corruption and social injustice

A picture of the rapid and stark stratification of Chinese society and the resulting dissatisfaction among various social sectors is not merely the consequence of disparities in income and access to services. Several other factors need to be considered too. The problems facing Xi Jinping and the entire CPC leadership are enormous.

One factor pertains to the slowing economy. As detailed in the next chapter, by the time Xi ascended to power in 2012, it had become clear that China's phenomenally fast economic growth would be unsustainable as China transitioned from an investment-led to a consumption-led growth model. The slowing economy has not – at least yet – had a great impact on those already in the workforce. But youth unemployment is a growing worry, with about

24 million young people hoping to enter the workforce each year. About half of them are college graduates, who complain of unsatisfactory job prospects and declining opportunities for upward mobility, which the reform decades provided in abundance.[14]

A second factor is corruption, which by 2012 had seeped into every aspect of life in China. Corruption has been regularly singled out in surveys as a top concern among Chinese people from every socioeconomic group. Corruption is recognised by both the government and citizens as a rot which not only contributes to ineffective governance and economic losses, but also is a mortal threat to the political system. It is the pervasive corruption of the ruling elites which many people inside and outside of China have predicted will eventually lead to the demise of the Party.

For decades, senior leaders have acknowledged corruption to be a serious problem. It fundamentally challenges CPC legitimacy. Already during the ten years of leadership by Xi's predecessor, Hu Jintao, older-generation Chinese described corruption as more prevalent than under Kuomintang (KMT) rule, before the founding of the PRC. Hu warned that corruption 'could cause the collapse of the party and the state'. Hu's predecessor, Jiang Zemin, stated 'corruption is the cancer' that could doom the Party and the socialist modernisation drive. Xi in turn declared, 'If we cannot manage the Party and govern it strictly ... our Party will sooner or later ... be consigned to history.'

It is important to understand what widespread corruption means for ordinary Chinese. Abuse of public office for private gain had become so insidious by 2012 that one could not go about everyday life without paying a bribe. Even books printed and distributed by state-sanctioned publishing houses that examine the scope of corruption in society describe in detail the customary sums to be paid to an employee of the state for just doing their job: for example, to a teacher to recommend that a toddler be accepted by a well-regarded preschool; to a lecturer to pass a graduation thesis; to a university professor to approve a master's degree; to a clerk to provide a stamp on a work permit or a business registration; to an office manager to approve a company tax declaration or an export licence; to a doctor to ensure that they prescribe a specific brand of medicine; to a manager to ensure promotion in any state-run work unit, such as a research institution, a clinic, a library, a design centre or a factory; or by an officer in the PLA to his superior officer to secure promotion to a higher rank or to a job leading to promotion.

In the early 1990s, securing approval from the local electricity bureau after the installation of an air conditioner in a privately owned apartment in a Beijing suburb cost the price of a lunch (about 50 RMB) with the person in control of the stamp to certify that the installation had been done correctly. By 2012 the price for this same minor approval had risen to 500 RMB, in cash, delivered discreetly in an envelope to the clerk in charge of the stamp. These are small-scale everyday examples. Large commercial transactions could entail exorbitant sums and favours including the purchasing of property, jewellery or fine wines and transferring cash or other assets overseas.

Alongside public dissatisfaction with corruption is the revulsion for social injustice felt by many Chinese citizens. One can openly talk about corruption, which can be seen as a form of social injustice in the way it advantages the few over the many. But there are other forms of social injustice which are off limits in public discussion – those that relate to the abuse of power suffered by ordinary citizens. Unjust treatment by those in authority is a common complaint. Those in positions of power such as the police or the judiciary often fail to fulfil their obligation to protect ordinary citizens. Moreover, ordinary citizens feel they are unable to obtain redress when they have been treated unjustly.

The rank or position held by an accused person can often determine the type of punishment or even the verdict a judge metes out. The status of a person's family can also determine whether one is called out by university authorities for cheating on an exam. Whether a driver is fined for running a red light sometimes depends on the 100 RMB bill the driver slips into the palm of a police officer, but sometimes it also depends on the social standing of the culprit.

An illuminating example of the sense of entitlement among privileged members of society is the 2010 case involving a senior police official named Li Gang and his son. The son, who was arrested for reckless driving leading to the death of a pedestrian, became infamous for warning the arresting policeman that 'My father is Li Gang!'[15] The incident was reported on social media and went viral. Despite Li Gang's attempts to settle the matter out of court with the deceased pedestrian's family, and the propaganda authorities' attempts to silence the public outcry, the young man was ultimately tried and sentenced to six years in prison. Today the phrase 'My father is Li Gang' is synonymous with an enduring belief that the powerful can flout the same rules which ordinary people must obey. Increasingly, the privileged are the inner-circle members, especially the children of relatively senior government officials and the super-rich. The official propaganda apparatus has unearthed a speech given at an anti-graft conference by Xi Jinping when he was a provincial official: 'Rein in your spouses, children, relatives, friends and staff, and vow not to use power for personal gain.'[16]

Public trust of the government's regulatory bodies is low. There is great scepticism among all sectors of Chinese society about the ability of the authorities to guarantee safe food or medicine, even though there are robust quality and inspection regulations in place for food, medicine and other health-related products. But enforcement is lacking. In 2008, 300,000 infants became ill from being fed milk powder contaminated with the toxic industrial compound melamine, leading to six fatalities. The scandal caused widespread public outrage, prompting the government to promulgate a Food Safety Law the following year that prohibited the use of unauthorised food additives. Public confidence in the regulatory bodies was further undermined after a vaccination scandal in March 2016 involving the illegal sale of improperly stored or expired drugs.

Chinese living in the countryside probably suffer most from the arbitrary abuse of power. Many aspects of their everyday existence depend on the goodwill and integrity of village officials. Villagers are in a weak position when confronted by abusive officials who demand arbitrary or unofficial taxes, levies and many types of miscellaneous fees. They have little legal recourse if their health and wellbeing is damaged by shoddy goods and services. They are also in a weak position when officials decree that their family plot is needed for a village enterprise. One prevalent and deep-seated grievance among countryside dwellers is the minimal compensation they have been offered for land reclaimed by authorities. In urban areas, too, many families have expressed bitter feelings about unfair or inequitable compensation for homes torn down to make way for roads, light-rail lines, shopping malls or other types of property development proposed by unscrupulous developers.

The war against corruption

In the months before Xi was anointed China's top leader, diverse elites – officials, businesspeople and intellectuals – were deeply worried about the future of their country. In part the anxiety was to be expected. In the run-up to the pivotal CPC Party Congress of 2012, speculation about the new leaders and their policies was rife. Power transitions throughout the reform period have caused unease among elites who worry about what the changes will mean for them. In part the pessimistic political mood was a result of daunting domestic problems, which only added to the uncertainty about China's ability to continue to prosper despite the remarkable rise in living standards over the past decades. The pace of economic growth was slowing, corruption was rampant, pollution was literally choking urban residents across the country, and political reform was moribund. But there seemed to be no consensus on how to even begin to inject accountability into governance mechanisms. Many elites agreed that bold reform would be necessary but were sceptical that the new CPC leader would have the political courage to embrace genuine change.

Upon taking over from Hu Jintao as General Secretary of the CPC and Chair of the Central Military Commission in November 2012, Xi Jinping moved to rapidly assert control over decision-making processes – more rapidly than anyone had envisioned. He swept aside many of the principles of collective leadership adhered to since China's last strongman, Deng Xiaoping, stopped wielding power in the early 1990s. Deng had endorsed the principles of collective leadership because he was adamant that no one man should be allowed to amass an excessive amount of power without checks and balances, as had happened during the Mao Zedong era. During the terms of Xi's predecessors, the CPC general secretary ensured political unity by balancing factional differences among his fellow Politburo Standing Committee members. Building consensus – or at least the perception of consensus – in the formulation of policy and the approval of senior appointments was the principal work of the general secretary.

Xi consolidated his authority by establishing new decision-making bodies with extensive power and with himself as chair. For example, Chinese analysts have described the new Central Leading Group for Comprehensively Deepening Reforms as more powerful than any government ministry. Xi has also taken the chair position in many more CPC leading small groups (LSGs) – informal interagency decision-making bodies – than the general secretary has previously done. Xi heads LSGs in charge of finance and the economy, national security, foreign affairs, Taiwan affairs, internet security, and military and defence reform. As with Politburo Standing Committee meetings, the deliberations of the LSGs are not made public.

Xi made it clear from the start that restoring people's faith in a revitalised Party was fundamental to rejuvenating the Chinese nation. As the son of a revolutionary leader, Xi belongs to the faction of 'red princelings' who view themselves as the true defenders of the Communist legacy. It is noteworthy that most of the new bodies established by Xi were placed within the CPC framework rather than within the government hierarchy.

Xi's emphasis on the need for the Party to reinvigorate its mandate is also evident in his guidelines called the Four Comprehensives: comprehensively build a moderately prosperous society, comprehensively deepen reform, comprehensively govern the nation according to the rule of law, and comprehensively and strictly govern the Party. Time and again Xi has called on CPC members to serve as genuine role models for honest hard-working citizens. Xi has encouraged the entire populace to pursue the China Dream by following 'twelve core socialist values' as defined by the Party, including prosperity, democracy, civility, patriotism and integrity.

As one of his first major initiatives, Xi launched a ferocious anti-corruption campaign. He appointed fellow Politburo Standing Committee member Wang Qishan to head it. Wang is respected both within and outside of China for his competence and perseverance. Former American secretary of the Treasury Henry Paulson has called Wang Qishan a man of great resolve and courage, one who has been fighting corruption for years.[17] According to one of many political jokes circulating in Beijing, a key reason that Wang is squeaky-clean is because he and his wife have no kids. Children of senior officials are viewed as among the most serious offenders when it comes to bribes and other abuses of their privileged position.

Xi's ongoing anti-corruption campaign has differed in several ways from previous campaigns. Xi's campaign has lasted longer than earlier ones and certainly longer than anyone expected. Furthermore, officials at all levels have been punished. Former Politburo Standing Committee member Zhou Yongkang became the most senior official since the founding of the PRC to be tried and convicted of corruption-related charges. An internal investigation concluded that Zhou abused his power, maintained extramarital affairs with multiple women, took massive bribes, exchanged money and favours for sex, and 'leaked state and party secrets'.[18] By March 2016, some 282,000 officials had been punished for 'discipline violations', a term used to indicate suspicion of corruption as well as breaking other rules, from living extravagantly to being lazy on the job.[19] Of these, 82,000 faced severe punishment.[20] Wang reported that ninety senior officials were investigated in 2015.[21] As of November 2016, the *ChinaFile* website of the Asia Society showed that since the start of the campaign, 184 top civilian officials, dubbed 'tigers', have been named in cases involving 2.7 billion RMB.[22] Another 1696 lower-level officials, called 'flies', have been named in cases worth 4.6 billion RMB.[23]

Corruption within the military has also been targeted. Dozens of senior military leaders have been publicly named as targets of investigation, including two former vice-chairmen of the Central Military Commission, Guo Boxiong and Xu Caihou, and eleven other senior military officers.

What do Chinese people think of the anti-corruption campaign? While it is impossible to fully gauge public opinion in a country that restricts freedom of expression, in Western media the campaign has been described as key to Xi's popularity among ordinary people.

No doubt ordinary people are happy to see officials being punished for spending public funds for personal pleasure. However, this judgement needs to be tempered with an acknowledgement that while anti-corruption measures are for the most part popular in China, many ordinary Chinese are politically savvy and cynical when it comes to appraising their leaders' intentions. This scepticism runs deep. A blog post called 'Why Xi's anti-graft campaign bores me' reflects popular sentiment. The post begins: 'I respect Wang Qishan's character and sense of responsibility as a government official. However, I have no interest whatsoever in the ongoing anti-corruption campaign.' The post's author goes on to list eight reasons. First, however long it lasts, the campaign will only deal with the tip of the iceberg: 'There are virtually "no non-corrupt officials!'" Second, 99 per cent of ousted officials are small fry. Third, official embezzlement figures are far smaller than the numbers circulating online. Have the real figures been purposefully covered up for fear of public outrage? Fourth, no one, no matter how corrupt, will be sentenced to death – despite the death penalty being used quite frequently in China. 'Corruption harms the entire nation and its people – at least all the common folk. It poisons the ethics and the heart of society.' Fifth, people have not seen a cent of the dirty money. 'Where is all that confiscated money going? Shouldn't the people be given a public account of how it's being used?' Sixth, corruption cases pointed out over the years by the people have not been investigated. 'A country with such a lack of transparency leaves its people completely in the dark.' Seventh, corrupt officials are treated to a quality of life in prison that most people could never hope to have in a lifetime. Lastly, whatever the anti-corruption campaign achieves, the result will always be more corruption than before.[24]

Of course, not everyone supports the crackdown on corruption. Critics include people involved in industries that used to profit from officials being treated to luxury goods – watches, jewellery, designer handbags – and those who benefited from officials being wined and dined, and treated to travel. Public servants – those in jeopardy from the anti-corruption campaign and fearful of losing their jobs or being jailed – are the ones who are the most disgruntled.

There are also signs that public confidence in the campaign is waning. A study conducted by Ni Xing and Li Zhu from Sun Yat-sen University in Guangzhou found that the higher the number of reported graft cases in a prefecture, the more people started to question the central government's failure to manage the localities.[25] Survey findings of this kind have raised doubts about the campaign's effectiveness.

There have been foreign media reports of economic stagnation in the provinces due to the reluctance of local government officials to make decisions or take actions that may draw attention to them, and thereby make them the target of investigation. However, some respected US-based China watchers – for example Cheng Li of The Brookings Institution – reject the notion that leaders have been dissuaded from making decisions. Li notes that officials will ultimately be removed from office if they fail to produce economic growth.[26] He also writes that official misbehaviour has decreased because officials fear being caught for any wrongdoing. Anecdotal evidence from three provinces in August 2016 also confirms that the anticorruption campaign at least has had a marked effect on conspicuous consumption by officials.

Harsh measures could erode support

Xi is undoubtedly powerful. Some liken him to Mao Zedong – and they note that Mao also created powerful CPC bodies to circumvent the bureaucracy and centralise decision-making. Xi has certainly built up a quasi cult-like aura around his persona, portraying himself as a popular and caring leader. He has promoted the need for social fairness and justice on numerous occasions, for example in his 2016 New Year address. Rap songs and online videos about 'Xi Daddy' – and 'Peng Mama', Xi's wife, singer Peng Liyuan – attract an audience of hundreds of millions.

Yet it is unclear how much support Xi enjoys and how popular he genuinely is among vital constituencies, among the other 89 million CPC members, as well as among government officials and the employees of state-run work units.

Even his popularity among ordinary citizens is not certain. In contrast to the anti-corruption campaign, which enjoys general public support, many of Xi's other measures pit him against popular sentiment. Five key measures, which have either been endorsed publicly by Xi or embraced by other senior officials, have not only upset intellectuals but also infuriated various other sectors of society.

One such measure is the beefed-up surveillance mechanism which has grown to support Wang Qishan and the powerful anti-graft task force he heads. Officially called the Central Commission for Discipline Inspection (CCDI), this agency previously dealt with intra-party disciplinary measures in a quiet and non-public way. Since early 2016, the CCDI has stationed inspectors in central Party and government departments. In addition to monitoring graft and pinpointing measures to reduce waste, the CCDI has become a kind of 'thought police' for officials, academics and professionals, denouncing anyone who they feel is disloyal to the Party leadership.

In an article about the CCDI, an official newspaper run by China's prosecutorial agency reminded readers of the Ming Dynasty body of imperial censors who hunted errant officials in the name of the emperor. Their special status and relationship with the emperor made these censors 'kings without crowns', the newspaper article noted, leaving little doubt that the powers bestowed by Xi to Wang and the CCDI are a source of concern to some within the system.[27] CCDI officials also enforce 'political discipline' in universities and colleges. In February 2016 the agency criticised the Party History Research Center for lacking 'a sense of responsibility in fighting historical nihilism'. It also questioned the Chinese Academy of Social Sciences for marginalising Marxism in certain academic disciplines.[28]

This attempt to instil ideological purity or correctness turns off even those middle-aged or older officials who wholeheartedly support anti-corruption measures. It certainly provokes either cynicism or outright indignation in younger officials. As for trying to dictate academic issues, Xi risks alienating academia entirely.

Another measure taken under Xi's watch which is bound to upset tens of millions of Chinese is the stricter surveillance by authorities of the internet and social media. In China there are thousands of websites that cannot be accessed because the content either has been deemed dangerous to political stability by the CPC Propaganda Department or contains a politically sensitive term like 'Dalai Lama'. Commonly referred to as the Great Firewall of China, the filter is so powerful that little escapes the censors. While attempts are made to get around the censorship, for the vast majority of internet users it is just a frustration they have to live with.

In addition, the discussions on dozens of chat rooms are constantly monitored so that they do not stray from politically correct topics. From time to time a blogger who has pushed the boundaries too far or too often is arrested and sentenced for inciting instability. This serves as a potent reminder of the authorities' ability to track down and punish individual internet users.

Middle-class and younger Chinese who travel abroad and are distinctly more international in mindset than their parents' generation particularly resent the Great Firewall of China. In 2015 the government declared that it was strengthening China's 'internet sovereignty' and reined in virtual private networks, which had been popular with Chinese web users to get around the Great Firewall and access services such as Google, Facebook and Twitter. According to Anne-Marie Brady, who for decades has studied CPC controls of political thought, 'only the likes of Iran, North Korea and Saudi

Arabia have a comparable level of internet censorship'.[29]

A third unpopular measure sanctioned by Xi pertains to the Chinese media, parts of which during recent decades began publishing thoughtful articles about a variety of topics with views that diverged from CPC orthodoxy. Intermittently, some of the more courageous editors allowed genuine investigative reporting about various social ills and irresponsible actions by local governments. In unequivocal terms, Xi has ordered the Chinese media to be loyal to the Party and restore people's trust in it. The key role of the media is not as speakers of the truth but 'disseminators of the Party's policies and propositions'.[30]

Fourth among the most unpopular of measures are the tougher security and surveillance laws that have been approved, including the National Security Law and the Law on Non-Governmental Organisations (NGOs). Since Xi came to power hundreds of rights activists, lawyers, journalists and writers have been harassed, detained and imprisoned. Intellectuals, including university faculty members, who during the Hu era could express mildly dissenting views on numerous sensitive topics, today receive warnings to remain silent or risk losing their jobs. The assault against differing or unorthodox stances is led by officials representing the CPC Propaganda Department, a Party organ that has wielded more political power since 2012.

In July 2015 more than 300 human-rights lawyers and activists were interrogated and intimidated, with twenty-two eventually arrested, fifteen of whom remain in detention, including two who started prison sentences in August 2016. According to the Network of Chinese Human Rights Defenders, their convictions make a mockery of justice. The defendants were denied basic due process and the right to a fair trial. The detainees had been held in secret locations, denied access to a lawyer of their own choice, and refused contact with their families. In a worrying new development, evidence presented to the court against a rights lawyer used a conversation he had had at dinner in a restaurant. Since the 1990s Chinese people have conversed in public places about even the most sensitive issues, based on the assumption that one can chat freely as long as one does not challenge the right of the Party to rule or publicly encourage others to rise up against it.

Fifth, during Xi's term propaganda authorities have zeroed in on 'dangerous Western thinking'. Despite the rise of nationalism in recent years, this does not resonate with broad sectors of Chinese society. Understandably, while most Chinese people are immensely proud of all that China has achieved in a mere three decades, they are also drawn to the West – either because it is different or because of the ideas and ideals that are forbidden in China.

In 2013 a secret CPC directive known as 'document no. 9' ordered its members to struggle against 'false ideological trends', including Western constitutional democracy; the belief that freedom, democracy and human rights are universal values; and the West's idea of the watchdog role of journalists. Institutions to push back against included Western embassies, consulates, media and NGOs.

Throughout the reform era there have been periods during which conservative ideologues have openly questioned the motives of Western and especially American engagement policies towards China. They have warned of hostile forces infiltrating Chinese society with the intention of undermining the Party's power. For example, after the global financial crisis they saw to it that Chinese media gloated over the havoc caused around the world to emphasise that

China must reject the pursuit of 'Western-style democracy'. A *People's Daily* editorial at the time summed this up by stating that democracy is looking more and more dysfunctional by the day and the Chinese political system is looking more and more advantageous.

Today, heightened vigilance against Western influence is once again guiding the Party's policies on the internet, traditional media, culture and entertainment, universities, think tanks and NGOs. For example, in 2016 the CCDI questioned several Chinese academics working on international issues about the benefits to be derived from their participation in overseas conferences. In these cases the CCDI did not suspect misuse of funds – the conference hosts had covered all travel expenses. Rather, these queries were driven by a suspicion that the academics were too enamoured with Western interpretations of international events. In another example reflecting the political atmosphere in Beijing, a Tsinghua University associate professor said in private conversation in late 2016 that his supervisor wished to draw senior policymakers' attention to their joint publication advocating that China stop even trying to gain respect from the West, 'as it will never happen'; rather, China should concentrate holistically and comprehensively on being the leader of the developing world. The associate professor is up for promotion and his supervisor, a well-known professor, wants to enhance his retirement package, so 'anything anti-West will be looked upon favourably'.

These kinds of warnings about the 'ideology of Western anti-China forces' have been common since the start of reform and opening. Xi's ideology-based campaign is not necessarily thoroughly anti-Western but rather an eclectic mixture of emphasising the superiority of Chinese culture and consolidating CPC authority while at the same time continuing to borrow from the West. Chinese leaders have been doing that for decades. What is new is the predominance of online blogs and social media as vehicles of communication in China. Of the many formidable challenges China's leaders face, one of the most difficult is managing the expectations of elites and ordinary citizens alike. The telecommunications revolution that has propelled China's economic rise has also made China a much more difficult place to govern and police. China is today a vibrant, complex society in which citizens have access to information in a manner unthinkable just ten years ago – despite the authorities' efforts to control flows of information. People express their views via social media and even in some instances in veiled forms via the official media. A popular way of criticising the government is with proverbs alluding to historical fables or true occurrences in imperial times, such as the 'kings without crowns' discussed earlier. Propaganda officials are continuously forced to create new methods and platforms to maintain control and censor content.

While much of the grousing of academics is distant from the everyday realities of middle-class Chinese, within both groups there are many who shun the anti-Western tone of Xi's ideological rhetoric. Despite disturbing nationalistic outbursts targeting Western culture on the internet, the younger generations in China especially remain fascinated by the West and are eager to learn about Western customs, including the ways Western societies function.

Will the Party last?

Ever since China embarked on reform and opening, observers have speculated on the question of when Chinese middle classes will deem strict political controls intolerable. When will they demand the right to speak freely, to publish freely and to influence policy-making via the ballot box? In other words, when will China follow in the footsteps of other fast-growing Asian economies that were previously ruled by harsh authoritarian governments – for example South Korea and Taiwan – and become a multi-party democracy? That question in turn has spurred speculation about whether a political transformation towards a more transparent, accountable and pluralist system of governance could occur in China peacefully or at least with minimal bloodshed, as it did in South Korea and Taiwan.

Before the Tiananmen movement of 1989, almost everyone in China agreed that the country needed to reform but senior officials differed on the pace of reform and the degree of importance attached to ideology. Some mid-career government officials, and many academics and intellectuals – even ordinary citizens – spoke loftily of China gradually moving towards democracy, the kind defined in Western terms as a parliamentary democracy, an independent judiciary to ensure the rule of law, freedom of speech and a free press. On the issue of elections, most reform-minded Chinese in the 1980s did not envision a gradual acceptance of multi-party but rather multi-candidate elections. But what is important here is that innovative and inspired debates about the need to genuinely institutionalise democratic mechanisms took place in democracy salons and in CPC journals in major Chinese cities during 1987 and 1988 – years that are often referred to by Chinese as two of the most politically open in modern Chinese history.

Throughout its history the Party has upheld the goal of democracy. Tony Abbott is not the only Westerner to erroneously cheer upon hearing that China will become a democracy by 2050 – as Abbott did in 2014 after Xi Jinping's speech in the Australian parliament.[31] Though Deng Xiaoping famously said 'democracy is our goal', he did so with significant caveats that are still accepted by the Party today: importantly, Deng said China should never adopt 'Western democracy'. Deng specifically rejected a multi-party representative system with checks and balances of the executive, legislative and judicial branches of government because these 'constituted a monopoly of the capitalist class'.[32] Additionally, according to Deng, democracy had to be enacted under the leadership of the Party.

After 1989 and especially after the collapse of the Soviet Union, the tone of any public discussion about the suitability of parliamentary democracy for China changed sharply. The phrase 'walking the road of the Soviet Union' became synonymous with 'chaos' and 'turmoil'. Chinese leaders were jolted by the speed with which the Soviet Communist Party and the Soviet empire collapsed, not to speak of the prospect of death by firing squad, as was the fate of their fellow communist leader, Romania's Nicolae Ceauşescu.

As the 1990s progressed the authorities made sure any activity that might promote political reform was 'nipped in the bud', to quote CPC General Secretary Jiang Zemin. Not only officials who had been considered reform-minded in the 1980s but also middle-class Chinese who had aspired to a gradual transformation towards democracy dismissed democratic elections as unsuitable for China. Most Chinese who had succeeded in moving into the ranks of the wealthy and middle classes came to realise that the notion of 'one person, one vote' could lead to China's rural residents taking power. This might endanger middle-class citizens' privileges.

At the same time, crime became a concern, partly as a result of the increased freedom of movement and the influx of millions of rural residents into the cities to perform menial labour. Consequently, many urban Chinese said they now realised democracy would not work in China because of the large uneducated – and in the eyes of many urban Chinese, 'uncivilised' – rural population. Many favoured harsh administrative measures to control migration from the country-side to the cities. By the turn of the twenty-first century, middle-class and wealthy Chinese tended increasingly to speak of the need for a strong government which enforced law and order. This notion was reinforced by Chinese media throughout the 1990s, through reports highlighting the chaotic nature of Russian society, the plummeting income levels of Russian urbanites, alarmingly high crime rates and severe political instability.

The Soviet example still haunts China's leaders today. Shortly after becoming general secretary, Xi reportedly warned that the Communist Party of the Soviet Union had collapsed because 'nobody was man enough to stand up and resist' its downfall.[33] Additionally Xi said the Soviet failure was caused by a crisis in belief – the people had lost faith in the Communist Party. Xi later reportedly declared that 'beliefs and faith' are the 'calcium' CPC members needed and without them the Party would 'develop rickets'.[34]

Political instability is the Chinese leadership's nightmare. Chinese authorities are extremely anxious about street protests, regardless of whether demonstrators are agitated because of a local government's unpaid pensions or another country's actions. At any given moment the demonstrators could direct their criticisms to the Party's leaders and question their competence to, for example, safeguard China's national interests. Internet commentary bemoaning weak or incompetent leaders, common during an international crisis involving China, also causes jitters among Chinese authorities.

As described in this chapter, Xi Jinping and the Chinese leadership face tremendous hurdles. In addition to the overarching challenge of maintaining economic growth, they must find ways to decrease many types of growing inequality, counter corruption and social injustice, and increase the accountability of government officials, as well as decrease pollution and its devastating effects on human health. There are hundreds of millions of discontented Chinese citizens. In recent years there have been at least 100,000 protests in China annually, involving a total of tens of millions of people.

Generally, the greatest source of discontent is the unfairness in Chinese society caused by the lack of an independent judiciary and the rule of law. Before Xi took power, many intellectuals and some officials identified far-reaching legal reform and major structural changes in the financial sector as prerequisites for continued economic growth. An independent judiciary would also curb corruption and social injustice. While in 2012 there seemed to be a general consensus among Chinese officials that legal reform was necessary, there were significant disagreements on the specifics of these reforms. Powerful interest groups, upon which the Party relies for political support, did not – and still do not – want to see their privileges eroded.

Xi's strong support of the far-reaching and ongoing anti-corruption campaign should be seen as a sign that he has the courage to challenge some vested interests. However, whether Xi is courageous enough to allow a genuinely independent judical system, one in which the Communist Party is not above the courts, remains to be seen. It is highly unlikely. But without judicial independence, genuine rule of law will not emerge – and many of the sources of discontent will not be addressed.

It is therefore pertinent to ask if pent-up frustration could reach a breaking point with huge numbers of people taking to the streets to demand more fair and competent rulers. As long as the economy continues to grow, it is not probable. As long as Chinese people perceive their situation today to be better than yesterday, and even more importantly, that the next generation will have a better life with greater opportunities, a grassroots, bottom-up, nationwide political movement is highly unlikely. There is no alternative to the Party because of the draconian measures taken by the domestic security forces to wipe out any organised dissent. Increasing resources have been invested in domestic security in recent years.

A political crisis could erupt for any number of reasons. If the economy falters, mass unemployment would create a volatile situation. In these circumstances, a horrific accident or natural disaster on par with the Fukushima catastrophe in Japan or an epidemic like the SARS virus could spiral out of control, severely threatening the health of Chinese citizens. If the Chinese government were to be widely perceived as incompetent in its response to such a major health crisis, one could foresee a dynamic leader emerging and appealing to the middle classes and the have-nots to join forces to challenge the established order. What the PLA would do in such a situation would be decisive.

Since the Tiananmen crisis in 1989, foreign observers have warned of the Party's fragility. Those predicting the coming collapse of either the CPC or China itself have been proven wrong time and again. The Party has consistently proven its resilience and its ability to deepen reform. Even while Xi is tightening CPC control over many aspects of society, he is encouraging intra-Party reforms to strengthen surveillance of CPC members. Although this will not solve some of China's serious governance problems, it would be hasty to view Xi's inflexible and harsh approach to political reform as a static state of affairs. Throughout the reform era, a few years of tightened control have been followed by some years of slightly looser constraints on intellectual, press and other freedoms.

Leadership matters. Many pivotal decisions are still to be made. Who Xi anoints in late 2017 to the all-powerful Politburo Standing Committee will be an important indicator of his intentions with regard to genuine reform. Five of the seven committee members are slated to retire at the nineteenth CPC Party Congress. Probably two of the new members will belong to the generation born in the 1960s: since their formative years China has been on the path of reform, open to the outside world, and in the throes of the telecommunications revolution, and during most of their adult life Chinese people have been bent on earning money.

Analysts both inside and outside China are as divided as ever in their predictions about the country's future. Some contemplate the effect of continuing repression, possibly even a harsher form than what we see in China today. Others view gradual change as possible – perhaps even probable – under pressure from a combination of forces. These include business leaders who demand financial reform and that market forces be more dominant, the ever-larger middle class that wants social justice, and the legal community that has a suite of reforms and more far-reaching checks and balances ready to put in place.[35] Those who view this as a distinct possibility emphasise that while Xi will do his utmost to ensure that the Party stays in power, he is also intent on going down in history as a transformative leader.

3.

CHINA'S ECONOMIC TRANSITION
Will it succeed?

Changes ahead

China's explosive growth has been one of the most remarkable economic stories of the past three decades. With an average annual real gross domestic product (GDP) growth rate of about 10 per cent from 1980 through 2013, China rose from a relatively impoverished backwater to become the world's second-biggest economy and largest trading nation.

Especially after 2000, its integration into global manufacturing production chains and massive investment in infrastructure and housing had a major impact on the relative prices of globally traded goods. Chinese demand drove up the prices of commodities such as iron ore, copper and coal five- to ten-fold, providing sustained windfall gains to commodity-exporting countries such as Australia.

Conversely, China's low labour and capital costs drove down the prices of its consumer goods exports. This also produced a mix of benefits and costs: consumers throughout the world enjoyed welfare gains thanks to the greater affordability of goods ranging from personal computers to motor scooters, but workers in high-wage locations suffered job losses and reduced wages as production was outsourced to China. China's unusually high rate of national saving, which peaked at around 50 per cent of GDP, also had an important global impact by pushing down interest rates. This arguably contributed to the United States's housing bubble of 2003–2007, which in turn helped precipitate the global financial crisis of 2008.

All of these global effects resulted not just from China's growth, but from the *style* of its growth: investment-intensive and focused on the installation of infrastructure, basic industries, export-oriented manufacturing capacity, and housing for the fast-swelling urban population. Since about 2013, however, China's growth model has begun an inexorable and permanent shift, and this shift has started to cause great changes in the nature of the nation's global impact.

Industrial production and construction have slowed dramatically, and the majority of China's GDP growth now comes from services and consumer spending. Demand for commodities has peaked and will probably decline in the coming decade. But appetite for international tourism and education is enormous and rising fast: China is now the world's biggest source of international tourists and its global tourism spending is now about one-third of the size of its annual trade surplus.

Finally, the nature of China's international investment flows is changing. Until about 2010, the large majority of China's outbound capital flows took the form of official reserve accumulation – purchases of US Treasury bonds and similar fixed-income instruments – by the People's Bank of China (PBOC). In recent years reserve accumulation slowed, and in 2015 reserves fell by more than US$500 billion. Meanwhile, other kinds of capital flows have increased markedly: outward direct investment by Chinese companies, infrastructure lending by state policy banks (which now handily exceeds the annual lending by the World Bank and other multilateral development banks), and portfolio investments by wealthy individuals.

In short, China is in the midst of big changes: shifting from an economy mainly dependent on capital spending to one mainly reliant on consumer spending. As a result, the nature of its economic influence on the rest of the world is changing accordingly. This shift is still in its early stages and will take a decade or more to complete. Moreover, there is no guarantee that the transition will be successful, with success defined as continued rapid growth in per capita income. It is possible that China could fall into the low-growth pattern (sometimes called the middle-income trap) that became the fate of many formerly high-powered Latin American and South-East Asian economies.

To avoid that outcome, Chinese leaders must undertake extensive reforms to its economic system. Boiled down to their essence, these reforms must encourage economic actors to move away from maximising *capital accumulation* and towards maximising *capital productivity*. In other words, if the task of the last three decades was to increase the amount of China's assets, the task of the coming decades is to increase the return on those assets. The policies China's leaders pursue will have enormous implications for China's people as well as China's economic partners, not least Australia.

Rebalancing the imbalances: how far has China come?

China's growth since 1979 had three major sources. First, China successfully adapted the East Asian developmental state model pioneered by Japan and later emulated by South Korea and Taiwan.[1] This model starts with land reform to break up large estates (or, in China's case, communes) and distribute agricultural land to family farms, which in a labour-abundant country have much higher productivity. The surplus income generated by the farm sector is then captured by a state-directed financial sector, which ploughs it back into investments in infrastructure and basic industry. Finally, the state prioritises export-oriented manufacturing, which ensures continuous technological upgrading and productivity gains.

Second, the PRC gradually reallocated resources away from relatively unproductive state-owned enterprises to more productive private firms. Starting from close to zero in 1980, private companies today account for nearly half of China's exports, roughly two-thirds of industrial output and fixed asset investment, and around 85 per cent of urban employment.

A final source for growth was demographics. Between 1975 and 2010, China's dependency ratio – that is, the number of people of non-working age for every 100 people of working age – more than halved, from 80 to 35. A huge expansion in the labour force made it possible for China to carve out a strong position in low-cost, labour-intensive manufacturing. And the relatively low number of dependent children and retirees meant that China could maintain a very high savings rate, enabling high rates of investment in industry and infrastructure. Requirements for social spending on education, health care and pensions, conversely, were fairly low.[2]

These elements combined to generate and sustain very high economic growth rates. But nothing lasts forever. Starting with the global financial crisis, China has faced the need to make a transition to a new growth model. The East Asian developmental state pattern, with its emphasis on exports and investment, has clearly reached its limits. Reliance on exports peaked in 2006, when total export value hit 35 per cent of GDP and the current account surplus reached 10 per cent of GDP – figures that declined to 22 per cent and 3 per cent respectively in 2015. Reliance on investment spending peaked in 2013 at around 46 per cent of GDP, the highest capital formation rate ever recorded for a major economy.

Similarly, the demographic tailwind has reversed. The dependency ratio started to rise in 2010, entirely because of an increase in the number of people over the age of sixty-five. Today China has about six people of working age for every retiree, about the same as Japan in 1980. By 2040 it will have only two workers for every pensioner, the same ratio as Japan today.[3]

Finally, the pace of reallocation of resources from the state to the private sector has slowed considerably. Between 1997 and 2008 the number of SOEs fell by 60 per cent, as did the number of SOE workers. The private sector share of national fixed asset investment rose from around 10 per cent to over 50 per cent. Since 2008, however, the number of SOEs has grown by about a third, to over 150,000, and their total assets have risen from 130 per cent of GDP to 180 per cent. The private sector's share of fixed asset investment and other indicators continues to rise, but at a much more sluggish pace than before 2008.

An important reason for this shift was the massive economic stimulus program of 2008–2009, which greatly expanded credit to local governments and SOEs to boost the construction of housing and infrastructure. This bolstered the role of the SOEs, but it also removed much of the incentive for delivering a high return on investment. As a result, the financial efficiency of SOEs has declined markedly: in 2015, industrial SOEs earned a return on assets of just 3 per cent, about one-third of the figure for private companies.

In short, the growth model that has served China so well over the last three decades is now reaching the end of its useful lifespan, and it must gradually be replaced by a new growth model. The simplest way of characterising the necessary transition is that China must move from an era of capital accumulation to an era of capital productivity.

Over the last few years, it has become clear that this transition from a capital-intensive growth model to a more services- and consumer-oriented growth model is well underway. The service sector share of GDP has risen steadily and now exceeds 50 per cent; the industrial share has shrunk and is now at 41 per cent. The investment share of GDP has peaked and has begun to decline, albeit glacially. Along with the peaking of investment demand, demand for basic materials and commodities – notably iron ore, coal, steel and other industrial metals – has also begun to decline. Consumer spending, on the other hand, remains resilient, and continues to grow at an annual rate of over 7 per cent, faster than the economy as a whole.[4]

But the transition is far from complete and there are serious concerns about the sustainability of growth at anything close to its 2015–2016 trend rate of around 6.5 per cent. The main issue is that the economy-wide return on capital is falling, dragged down by the deteriorating returns in the SOE sector. Recent work by the Organisation for Economic Cooperation and Development (OECD) found that between 2000 and 2007, China's economic growth came about equally from capital accumulation and productivity gains, which is about what one would expect during a high-speed capital accumulation era. Between 2008 and 2012, productivity gains accounted for just a quarter of GDP growth on average, and by the end of that period productivity contributed only one-sixth of growth.[5]

In other words, instead of becoming more reliant on productivity gains to power its growth, as it needs to do, China is increasing its dependence on simply adding more investment. Much of this relatively unproductive investment is financed by debt, with the result that the nation's gross debt to GDP ratio rose from 140 per cent in 2008 to 249 per cent in 2015. The gross debt of China's corporate sector is now around 160 per cent of GDP, one of the highest ratios in the world.

This reliance on low-productivity, debt-financed investment is clearly unsustainable. If current trends continue unabated, it is likely that China's debt burden will trigger either a financial crisis or a severe growth slowdown by 2020 at the latest, and quite possibly sooner. To avert this outcome, strong policies are required to boost productivity growth. The government outlined such a policy agenda in 2013, but so far implementation has been sluggish.

Lack of progress

In November 2013, the Third Plenum of the eighteenth Party Congress of the CPC issued a decision document that laid out a comprehensive economic reform agenda. A signature slogan from the decision was that 'market forces should have a decisive role in resource allocation'.

The main elements of the Third Plenum decision were:

- Financial liberalisation, to make the allocation of capital less political and more market-driven

- Fiscal reform, to restructure the burgeoning debt of local governments, to reduce the reliance of localities on land sales and production taxes, and to create incentives for local governments to promote services and consumer-oriented sectors

- An ambitious program of industrial upgrading, which was later spelled out in more detail in the 'Made in China 2025' industrial policy plan released in 2015

- A restructuring of SOEs built around the concept of 'mixed ownership', which at the time was interpreted to mean the introduction of private shareholders.

The reforms were widely hailed as an ambitious set of policies well-designed to help China manage the transition from a capital-mobilisation to a capital-efficiency economy. However, since the November 2013 decision was issued, the prognosis has soured. Progress on the main reform initiatives has been spotty at best, and in some areas close to non-existent. The most progress has occurred in the financial arena, but at a high cost in market disruption and erosion of the market's belief in the competence of policymakers. Fiscal reform has succeeded in ending local governments' reliance on land sales but it has failed to stop the increase in local government borrowing.

Perhaps most important, virtually nothing has been done to restructure the SOEs, which lie at the heart of China's productivity problem since (as explained above) their return on assets is far lower than that of private firms, and in steady decline. Plans to introduce private shareholders have effectively been abandoned, and 'mixed ownership' now seems to mean little more than giving state firms new state-owned shareholders.

There are two main explanations for these disappointing results. The more optimistic one is that Xi Jinping and his colleagues are genuinely committed to productivity-enhancing reforms, but have found both the technical difficulties and the political obstacles to implementation far greater than they anticipated.

If this interpretation is correct, then one would expect to see some acceleration in the pace of economic reforms after the CPC Congress in late 2017. This is because that Congress will see the replacement of five of the seven members of the Politburo Standing Committee, and about two-thirds of the Party's Central Committee. Xi will have a major if not decisive influence in picking this new leadership line-up. In principle he will then be in a much stronger political position to push through difficult or controversial reforms.

The pessimistic interpretation is that Xi is less committed to a productivity agenda than he is to maximising the state's control over the economy, or that his economic policies are simply confused. Although not conclusive, the evidence for this view is mounting.

This problem does not relate merely to the management of the SOEs. It affects every aspect of the relationship between state and market. Efforts to increase the role of market forces are severely constrained by the desire of the state to override market outcomes that it views as undesirable for one reason or another. This is evident in the watering down of SOE reform, where the original plan of introducing private shareholders was apparently judged to pose too much of a risk to state control. But it is also salient in the area where reforms seem to have made the most progress: the financial sector.

On the surface, progress on financial reform has been impressive. Deposit interest rates were formally deregulated in June 2015, and by the end of the year the renminbi had been moved off its longstanding US dollar peg and into a trade-weighted targeting mechanism. Foreign investment quotas on the domestic stock market were substantially raised, and foreign investors were also given access to the Shanghai market via Hong Kong brokerage accounts under the Shanghai-Hong Kong Stock Connect program. In early 2016 foreign investors gained access to the interbank bond market, by far the largest of China's three bond markets. All these reforms are designed to make the allocation of capital more market-driven and to increase competition in the financial sector.

But the impact of these reforms has been offset by heavy-handed government intervention in both the equity and foreign exchange markets. China's stock market experienced a mini-bubble in late 2014 and early 2015, as local investors borrowed heavily to bid up stocks, perhaps on the expectation that reforms would bring in foreign buyers, driving stock prices even higher. The government actively encouraged small investors to pile in, even though the market is poorly regulated and subject to wild swings.

When the bubble popped in June 2015, stock prices plunged. Rather than letting the market return by itself to a more rational level, the central government suspended trading for many issues, and organised a massive buying program by SOEs and state-controlled investment funds. This extraordinary intervention to support equity prices at a level that was politically expedient, but not obviously related to their market value, made many observers wonder how deep Beijing's commitment was to letting market forces have 'a decisive role in resource allocation'.

These doubts intensified in August, when without warning the PBOC devalued the renminbi by about 2 per cent, and announced that the currency's opening rate each day would be determined by the previous day's market close, rather than arbitrarily as in the past. This appeared to be a move towards a more market-determined exchange rate, but the PBOC was quickly forced to backtrack, as the surprise devaluation triggered panic selling of the currency by traders who believed that further devaluation might be on the way. To stabilise the exchange rate, the PBOC started selling billions of US dollars each day to buy up renminbi. This tactic ultimately succeeded in keeping the exchange rate stable, but as with the earlier stock market episode, observers were left wondering what had become of the government's commitment to market prices.

Finally, regulators repeated their errors in early January 2016. The securities regulator introduced a poorly designed 'circuit breaker' rule designed to stop stock market volatility by suspending trading once stock prices moved more than 5 per cent in one day. Instead of stabilising the market, it induced panic selling, and stock markets around the world also fell sharply in response.

At the same time, the renminbi came under renewed pressure, thanks to a vaguely worded statement on the PBOC website indicating that the central bank would no longer manage the currency against the US dollar, but rather against a currency basket. Traders read this as camouflage for a major devaluation to boost a flagging economy – a not unreasonable interpretation, given the turmoil on the stock market and generally weak economic data. This prompted another two months of heavy PBOC intervention on foreign exchange markets to stabilise the currency.

The end result of all this activity is confusion. There is no clarity on the basic direction of policy: does Beijing want a greater role for market forces, or not? It seems clear that Xi feels no urgency to resolve this contradiction at any point before the 2017 Party Congress.[6]

Future growth scenarios

There are many possible trajectories for China's economic future. For analytical clarity, it is convenient to consider two basic scenarios. The first assumes that some package of productivity-enhancing reforms is enacted between now and 2020, enabling the GDP growth rate to stabilise at around 5 per cent or perhaps a bit higher, while the gross debt to GDP ratio stabilises at somewhere around 300 per cent, similar to that of the United States. Under these conditions China would be well placed for a very successful decade in the 2020s. The second scenario assumes that reforms are inadequate, in which case either a financial crisis or a severe downturn in growth becomes likely by 2020 at the latest.

What would success look like?

This scenario assumes either that Xi is biding his time until after the 2017 Party Congress to focus on structural economic reform, or that economic fragility becomes so apparent by late 2017 or early 2018 that the leadership feels compelled to overcome its nervousness and push for aggressive market-friendly measures.[7] Under this scenario, between 2017 and 2020, a reasonable proportion of the following is achieved:

- Excess capacity in heavy industry (especially coal and steel) is decisively shut down, with the loss of approximately 5 million jobs

- Non-strategic SOEs controlled by local governments are restructured by a combination of bankruptcies, privatisation or reorganisation under more financially disciplined state shareholders, with another 5 million or so job losses, and a significant reduction in the level of SOE assets from their present level of about 180 per cent of GDP

- Significant deregulation of key service sectors – notably telecommunications, aviation, logistics, finance, health care and non-compulsory education – enables much more active participation by domestic private and foreign firms

- The country's banking system is recapitalised by the government, at a cost of roughly US$1 trillion or 7–8 per cent of GDP; bad loans in the banking system are hived off into asset management companies; the responsibility of commercial banks to lend to SOEs or local governments for policy purposes is reduced or ended; the practice of the government informally guiding banks on which sectors to lend to and at what rates is substantially curtailed

- Local government finances are fully restructured: localities are banned from bank borrowing and have their revenues restructured so that the majority comes from services, consumption taxes and taxes on the value of property

- The renminbi exchange rate moves to a Singapore-style trade-weighted basket peg and is allowed to move up and down in a relatively broad range with minimal central bank intervention.

Under this scenario, it is quite possible that the years 2018 to 2020 will see some reduction in the GDP growth rate, as millions of workers in non-competitive industries are laid off, and as credit growth slows substantially thanks to the financial restructuring that will restrict loans to local governments and the less efficient parts of the SOE sector. The government could offset these negative growth effects by increasing its explicit fiscal spending, although it would need to be careful to bias the fiscal impulse in favour of consumption-friendly items rather than the traditional infrastructure projects: cash transfers to laid-off workers and other low-income people, or greater healthcare and education spending.

The crucial outcome under the 'successful reform' scenario is that the climate for private sector investment improves substantially, and the private sector's share of nationwide fixed-asset investment rises from its current level of around 65 per cent to over 80 per cent. Because private firms will mainly pursue high-return investments in labour-intensive services, the household share of national income will rise, wage growth will remain robust, and there will be a solid foundation for an economy increasingly reliant on consumer demand.

Overall GDP growth would stabilise at around 5 per cent a year in the early 2020s – significantly lower than the current rate, but an extremely high rate for the world's second-largest economy – and about two-thirds of incremental GDP growth would come from consumer spending. As a result, the household consumption share of GDP would rise from its current level of 38 per cent to 45 per cent or more by 2025 and 50 per cent by 2030, a level that is more or less in line with other middle-income Asian countries.

At the same time, the national debt to GDP ratio would stabilise, at a high but manageable level. The composition of debt would change somewhat, with an increase in consolidated government debt (central and local combined) from the current 60 per cent of GDP to 80–85 per cent. The increase in formal government debt would be required by the bank recapitalisation and the bigger fiscal deficits required to sustain growth during the transition years of 2018 to 2020. Corporate debt might stabilise at close to 200 per cent of GDP by 2020, after which a slow deleveraging of the corporate sector would be offset by increased borrowing by households, whose debt load remains relatively light.

There is no question that achieving this outcome would be difficult, and would require far more commitment to deep reforms – and a much greater willingness to surrender state control in key parts of the economy – than the Xi government has shown so far. But it is by no means an unrealistic target.

And failure to reform?

Under this scenario, over the next few years growth steadily slows, and the debt to GDP ratio continues to rise rapidly, as the government desperately tries to support flagging growth by encouraging the banks to shovel more and more money into projects that deliver a lower and lower return. With growth and productivity sagging, and the debt level relentlessly rising, the economy loses its ability to muddle through, and something bad happens by 2020 or so.

There are various possibilities for what 'something bad' might be.[8] The one most frequently discussed is a financial crisis, triggered by runaway growth in non-performing loans. China is not likely to experience a classic developing-country balance of payments or currency crisis, because it runs a very robust current account surplus (about 3 per cent of GDP) and borrows relatively little from abroad in foreign currency. So China probably will not run into the kind of problem that engulfed Brazil and much of Latin America in the 1980s, or South-East Asia and South Korea in the 1990s, when foreign creditors triggered financial collapse by calling in their loans.

However, China could suffer a domestically generated financial crisis, caused by banks seeing their capital wiped out by rising losses on non-performing loans. Unless quickly checked by government action, failures of a few smaller banks could easily cascade into a much larger problem, if depositors lose confidence in the safety of their deposits and move en masse to take their cash out of the banking system.

Once the pressures in the financial system reach a crisis point, there are essentially two possible pathways. One is that the government ignores the warning signs until it is too late, and a full-blown financial crisis hits. Small and medium-sized banks fail, and even the bigger banks become unwilling to extend credit. Companies desperately sell assets to pay down the debts that their banks are unwilling to roll over, and asset prices collapse. The collapse in asset prices means that loans that once appeared healthy, because they were collateralised by high-value assets, are no longer healthy. More and more borrowers go into default, and more banks find themselves facing insolvency. Investment plummets, economic output contracts and unemployment soars.

This outcome is not very likely, since it assumes that the government will both ignore the warning signs before the crisis and be slow to act once the crisis starts unfolding. The first condition is possible but the second is not: in the global financial crisis of

2008–2009, China's government was caught off guard but then reacted very swiftly with an enormous fiscal stimulus program to stabilise growth. Given the Party's obsession with maintaining social stability at all costs, it is almost certain that it would react to a financial crisis with quick and massive countermeasures.

So the more likely pathway is not a sudden financial collapse, but a response similar to that in Japan after the bursting of the stock market and real estate bubbles in 1990. The government would step in quickly to bail out the vulnerable banks, and would instruct the bigger and healthier banks to keep lending to non-performing borrowers. This would in effect double down on the practice of supporting the economy by the extension of credit to non-productive uses.

Such a response would prevent a collapse of the banking system and an outright recession, but would most likely lock the country in to an extended period of GDP growth in the 0–2 per cent range, similar to Japan's 'lost decade' of the 1990s. As Japan has shown, so long as debt is in the local currency and held by domestic banks, it is perfectly possible for the debt to GDP ratio to keep rising, almost without limit, without precipitating a collapse of the financial system. The cost of such a strategy, however, is a virtually permanent condition of extremely low growth and steady deflation.[9]

International implications of the two scenarios
The optimistic case

The optimistic growth scenario is broadly positive for China's trade and investment partners, but carries some political risks. A China growing steadily at 5 per cent in the 2020s, with a rising share of growth coming from consumer spending, would obviously create huge new potential markets for firms selling more sophisticated consumer goods and services. These would include leisure, tourism, health care, education and financial services, for which Chinese demand is already large and fast-growing.

At least as significant would be an increase and diversification in China's outbound capital flows. On the direct investment side, the biggest increase would come from private firms. Some would look to increase their manufacturing presence abroad, closer to their final customers; others would look to acquire technology or distribution channels. On the portfolio side, a successful economic transition implies a major lowering of the capital controls that now prevent most ordinary Chinese from investing in overseas stock and bond markets. The introduction of a large pool of Chinese capital into global markets would almost certainly be very positive for many asset prices.

A successful China would also pose some significant challenges, some economic and some political. For one thing, it would almost certainly have a far larger number of globally successful private firms than it does today, and these would provide stiff competition for multinational incumbents across a wide range of industries.

In addition, some of the biggest SOEs would continue to be influential, and would also seek to expand their international presence. Since it is rarely clear to what extent SOEs are agents of a national strategic agenda set by the Party, and to what extent they are normal commercial actors, their increasing international investments would intensify the already serious national security concerns that many partner countries already have. Managing the domestic political response to large-scale Chinese investment, by both private and state firms, would be a major challenge for many governments.

Politically, it should not be assumed that a more prosperous China would also become a more open and pluralistic China, although that is a possible outcome. On the contrary, the legitimacy and authority of the Party may well be enhanced by economic success. As a result, it could well become far more aggressive in pursuing its goal of returning China to its 'rightful place' as a global superpower by 2049, the centenary of the Party's ascent to power.

Some aspects of this greater political assertiveness might be a bit uncomfortable for established players, but essentially benign. These include efforts to improve connectivity in Asia through the One Belt, One Road infrastructure program, and to create new multilateral funding channels via the Asian Infrastructure Investment Bank and the New Development Bank.

Other aspects would be quite a bit less benign, and would require some very hard strategic thinking. The most critical question of all is whether a successful China would remain content to keep embedding itself in a US-dominated system of global rules, or whether it would try to establish a China-centric order (at least in Asia) based less on rules and legal principles than on the raw fact of Chinese power. Over the last three decades China has been an assiduous joiner of most major international economic agreements and arrangements, and generally speaking it has played by the rules of these arrangements as much as any other major country.

On the other hand, it has rarely played a strong constructive and cooperative role in refining and improving these agreements, and there is little evidence of a trajectory towards more active participation. And behind the scenes, China is unabashed in using its economic leverage to threaten reprisals against countries that do not comply with its political demands (discussed further in Chapter 5).

The question then becomes whether conformance to an international rules-based system, however grudging, is a necessary condition for China's sustained economic success. In other words, does the 'successful China' scenario have embedded within it the requirement that China become a more fully cooperative member of the international economic community, however much its leaders may resent the constraints this puts on their political ambitions?

Another related question is whether the 'successful China' scenario contains an embedded requirement for significant political change. So far, predictions that economic development and modernisation would lead to a more liberal political regime have proved dismally wrong, so it would be unwise to be too bold in predicting the demise or substantive reform of the Party. But it may be that the successful transition to a more consumer-oriented economy compels a shift to a more pluralistic and open political system, much as it did in South Korea and Taiwan in the 1990s, and it may be that a stubborn refusal by the Party to open up the political process will doom China's hopes for sustained economic success.

An optimistic view, therefore, is that the 'successful China' scenario can only unfold if China becomes a more fully cooperative member of the international economic order, makes its political system more inclusive and open, and operates both domestically and internationally more by rules and less through the practice of *realpolitik*. In this case, a successful China may well create challenges and frictions in the Asia-Pacific and among its trade and investment partners around the world, but on balance it will be beneficial. A less positive view is that success in managing a difficult transition will enhance the legitimacy and power of a secretive Party that will seek to strengthen its authoritarian rule at home and its ability to exercise raw power abroad.

The pessimistic case

Economically, the consequences of an outright crisis in China, leading to a sudden plunge in demand, would be extremely damaging for the global economy: China is now a dominant import and/ or export partner for close to 100 countries.[10] By 2020 it will also be the leading source of external investment for many countries in the developing world. A sharp downturn in the Chinese economy, probably accompanied by a significant currency devaluation, might well be enough to put the entire world, or a substantial part of it, into recession.

Yet if, as seems more probable, the Chinese authorities pre-empt a dramatic crisis and instead preside over a slow, Japan-style stagnation, the impact could well be more subtle. Trade and investment flows would continue, and in fact China's more dynamic private sector firms could continue to expand their global footprint, much as the top Japanese companies did throughout the 1990s. The constraints on overseas infrastructure investment by state-owned enterprises would probably appear only gradually, and indeed it might be several years before it became clear that the tide of China's global influence was really ebbing.

The central question is what impact a long period of economic stagnation would have on domestic and international politics. There are two schools of thought. One holds that as economic growth slows and becomes less reliable as a guarantor of the Party's legitimacy, China's leaders would rely more on bellicose nationalism to shore up domestic political support. This outcome – in which China came more and more to resemble Vladimir Putin's Russia – would obviously be very destabilising for the Asia-Pacific region.

An alternative and in many ways more probable outcome is that when faced with an intractable and permanent economic downturn, China's leaders would turn inward rather than outward. Most important to the Party would be to ensure social and regime stability with a host of measures aimed at keeping the populace reasonably content: increased public-works spending to guarantee employment, increased social welfare spending, and increased repression and control of the media. This would be a more reliable way of ensuring legitimacy, rather than indulging in overseas adventures with a high risk of failure. As the costs – both in fiscal terms and in leaders' time – of this social stability maintenance project rose, China would probably slowly scale back its discretionary international engagements.

In some ways this outcome would be less worrisome and perhaps more attractive for the world's incumbent power holders, the United States and its allies. China's large market would continue to offer good opportunities for many companies, and China's accumulated wealth would still make it an important international investor. At the same time, the strategic threat of a geopolitically much more active China interested in displacing a rules-based economic order with a power-based one would disappear.

Yet the long-run costs to the world economy would be severe. As the world population ages, global economic growth is likely to slow, and new sources of vibrant demand will be in short supply. A successful China could be a sustained source of such demand for several decades, and provided the associated geopolitical tensions could be managed, this would be a large net positive for the world economy. A stagnant China would deprive the world of an important source of growth and innovation in the twenty-first century, and most nations – not just China – would be the poorer for it.

What will this mean for Australia?

For Australia specifically, the 'successful China' scenario harbours enormous economic opportunities, along with some political risks. Because of its strengths as a provider of educational and financial services, its attractiveness as a tourist destination, and its relative openness to foreign investment, Australia is well placed to benefit from the emerging sources of consumer demand and from increases in Chinese outbound portfolio and direct investment.

The only caveat to this generally positive picture is that commodities, which have been a key component of Chinese demand over the past fifteen years, and the single most important element of the Australia–China economic relationship, are already fading in significance and will continue to do so. The notion that Chinese-led infrastructure investment in Asia under the One Belt, One Road initiative can replace the demand lost from the Chinese housing market is fantasy: at the very outside, external infrastructure demand will be able to soak up no more than 10 per cent of the excess capacity that now exists in Chinese heavy industry.

It is critical, therefore, that Australian economic policymakers recognise that the China-led hard commodity boom is over for good. While Chinese volume demand will remain high for many years to come, it is unlikely to grow and thus will not produce any significant upward pressure on prices.

The outlook for energy is more mixed, since a successful China will see steadily increasing demand for transport fuel, and electricity demand is also likely to rise gradually as households take over from industry as the main consumers of power. Demand for oil (both crude and refined) is likely to keep growing at 1–3 per cent a year, and natural gas demand growth will also be strong as China continues its efforts to shift more of its power generation to gas-fired plants, and to replace household use of coal for cooking and heating with gas. On the other hand, demand growth for fossil fuels will be significantly constrained by the policy objectives of reducing the economy's overall energy intensity, and increasing reliance on renewable energy sources.

Finally, it would be wise to temper optimism about the prospects for Chinese agricultural imports. A common story is that as China's consumer affluence increases, diets will become richer and more meat-intensive, opening the door to a boom in imports of meat and feed grains. Yet the average Chinese diet is already very rich and meat-intensive. The average Chinese consumes about 3100 calories a day, the same as in South Korea. Looking ahead, it is also likely that a rapidly ageing China will follow the path of Japan, where the average daily calorie intake has declined over the past twenty years.

Assuming Chinese leaders will be able to pre-empt the worst outcomes of a severe downturn and instead manage a relatively benign, Japan-style slowing of the economy, Australia could expect to reap some benefit. For a small, open economy such as Australia's, this scenario is very favourable, because it would be well placed to take advantage of niche opportunities emanating from China, and could in fact benefit from increased flows of portfolio investment from Chinese individuals and institutions discouraged by the low returns available at home. In terms of the geopolitics, this assumes that

Chinese leaders are more likely to look inward to focus on political and social challenges at home, rather than turn to more aggressive external behaviour to bolster their domestic credibility. Clearly, an economically stagnating and more aggressive China poses the greatest risks for Australia, but is the least likely outcome at this stage.

Between 2003 and 2013, Australia's annual goods exports to China soared nineteen-fold, from A$5 billion to A$95 billion. The overwhelming driver behind this increase was exports of iron ore, which rose in volume terms from 64 million tons to 464 million tons, and in value terms from US$1.1 billion to US$51 billion. Other natural resources, notably copper, bauxite, oil and gas, enjoyed similar booms. By the peak of the China boom in 2013, China accounted for 32.5 per cent of Australian export value, up from 5 per cent a decade earlier. Minerals and fuels accounted for three-quarters of the value of Australian shipments to China; China was the market for nearly half of Australia's resource exports.

This boom was beneficial for the extractives industries and attracted large new investments – much of them from China – in mines and related infrastructure. But the consequent rise in the Australian dollar rendered much of Australia's manufacturing uncompetitive: manufactured goods fell from about 30 per cent of Australian export value in 2003 to just 16 per cent in 2013, and manufactured exports fell in absolute terms of A$48 billion in 2008 to an average of A$40 billion in the next four years. The initial decline resulted mainly from the collapse in global demand following the 2008 global financial crisis. But the subsequent failure to recover owed much to the loss of competitiveness due to an overvalued currency.

Looking ahead, it is probable that both the volume and the value of iron ore and other commodity shipments to China will remain roughly stable at around current levels. Imports can only rise substantially if there is a significant increase in demand. Such an increase is most unlikely: China's steel industry has excess capacity of around 200 million tons of annual production, and the country is coming under intense pressure from trade partners to shut down this excess capacity rather than export its excess production, as was largely the case in 2015–2016. Prices are likely to fluctuate around current levels for several years, as long as the global supply glut endures. So it would be unwise to base business strategy or policy on the rosy assumption that China will drive another long-term rebound in commodity demand or prices.

In fact, it might turn out that 2013 was the peak year for Australian export exposure to China. In that year, China accounted for 32.5 per cent of Australian export value, and 43 per cent of exports of minerals and fuels. By 2015 those shares were 33 per cent and 38 per cent respectively. In absolute terms, the value of Australian exports to China fell by 14 per cent in that period, from A$95 billion to A$81 billion. It is not realistic to hope that the long-term decline in hard (industrial) commodity exports will be fully offset by a rise in soft (agricultural) commodities catering to Chinese consumer demand: from 2013 to 2015, as the value of minerals and fuels exports to China fell by A$18 billion, the value of agricultural exports rose by less than A$2 billion. China's share of Australia's agricultural export value has remained roughly constant at around 20 per cent since 2012.[11]

A final consequence of the collapse of the commodities boom, according to the China Global Investment Tracker (CGIT) database, was a diversification of large-scale Chinese foreign direct investment (FDI) in Australia away from resource extraction and into technology, tourism, transport and real estate. From 2005 through 2013, Chinese firms made sixty-two direct investments valued at US$100 million or more in Australian projects and companies, with a total value of US$57 billion (US$44 billion if one excludes the exceptional case of Chinalco's purchase of a 10 per cent stake in Rio Tinto). Over 90 per cent of this investment was in energy or mining projects.

Large-scale Chinese FDI in Australia actually increased sharply in 2014–2015, to around US$11 billion a year, but only a third of this went into energy or mining; more than half went into stakes in technology, transport and real estate companies. A concerning development in this area is a sharp fall in large-scale Chinese FDI in the first half of 2016. This is most likely the result of China's tightening of controls on outbound capital flows, following a small currency devaluation and an episode of capital flight in late 2015. China has a super-abundance of domestic capital, and with investment returns at home in secular decline, there will be increased incentive for Chinese firms to diversify their investments abroad. But the sharp downturn in outward investment in 2016 is a salutary reminder of how easily Chinese capital flows can be cut off by abrupt and unpredictable changes in policy.

It is worth noting in this context that there is a substantial discrepancy between the CGIT data on Chinese FDI in Australia, and balance of payments data on inward FDI published by the Australian government, which generally show a lower level of Chinese inflows, and somewhat different annual patterns. According to government data, inflows of Chinese FDI into Australia totalled A$36 billion from 2006 to 2015, 8 per cent of all FDI in the country. Flows of all types of Chinese investment – including portfolio purchases of equities and debt securities – were A$70 billion during that decade, 6 per cent of all inflows.

Several factors likely contribute to this discrepancy. First, the CGIT data may categorise as direct investment some transactions classified as portfolio flows in the balance of payments. Second, CGIT does not remove from its database deals that are announced but subsequently cancelled. Finally, the balance of payments data may not attribute to China transactions done by Chinese firms via holding companies in other jurisdictions, such as Hong Kong or various tax havens.[12]

Despite these data problems, two overarching conclusions seem clear. First, Chinese investment in Australia has declined recently (although CGIT puts the peak year of Chinese inflows as 2015, whereas balance of payments data shows a peak in 2013). And second, despite all the headlines it has generated, China by no means dominates investment inflows into Australia. According to the balance of payments, China has accounted for only 6 per cent of total foreign investment in Australia in the last decade, and in only two years out of the ten did China account for more than 10 per cent of all inbound investment. Chinese investments account for only 2 per cent of the accumulated stock of more than A$3 trillion in inbound investment. So while a reduction in Chinese investment flows should be a source of concern, it is by no means a catastrophic event.

What steps for the future?

Adding up all these factors, it becomes abundantly clear that Australian economic policies should adapt to China's transition from an investment-driven, commodity-intensive economy to one driven more by consumer spending and services. What are some key steps on this pathway?

At the macro-economic level, there should be no assumption that Chinese consumer demand will ignite a boom in agricultural commodities. Rather, the focus should be on expanding Australia's comparative advantage in services, as opposed to reviving traditional manufacturing industries. Manufacturing comparative advantage remains overwhelmingly with China and its immediate Asian neighbours. Conversely, China's service trade deficit has expanded sharply since 2010, driven largely but not exclusively by a doubling in spending by Chinese tourists abroad. A services-oriented strategy offers three dimensions of opportunity for Australia to profit from China's transition.

The first is spending by Chinese individuals and companies on services in Australia. These service exports to China have grown steadily from A$1.3 billion in 2001 to A$10.7 billion in 2016. Tourism and education are the traditional mainstays, but quality health care and retirement care are likely to be important growth industries as China's population ages. Whether it is practically possible to have export-oriented versions of these services, catering to foreign cash-paying demand, alongside domestically oriented social services is an open question; these sorts of opportunities may be best exploited through direct investments in China.

The second would be direct investments in China, both in healthcare and retirement services as already mentioned, as well as in tourism and leisure facilities in which Australian firms have established expertise, and in financial and legal services. The obstacle here is not consumer demand – which is growing rapidly across all categories – but regulatory obstacles. China has a fairly open regime for FDI in manufacturing, but is by a wide margin the most closed major economy in the world when it comes to FDI in services. Taking advantage of opportunities in China's services sector will require intensive diplomacy to reduce some of these barriers.

A third area is Chinese FDI in services in Australia. Chinese firms have made a handful of large-scale direct investments in Australian transport and tourism assets in recent years (entirely through mergers and acquisitions activity rather than greenfield investment). This activity is likely to increase as Chinese firms look to develop China-oriented tourism and leisure projects in attractive destinations, and this should be welcomed.

Turning to trade and investment policy, the benefits from rising Chinese consumer demand for modern services will require extensive diplomatic efforts to crack open the Chinese market. The market for health care, education, leisure, financial, legal and other professional services in China is enticing, but in almost all instances these sectors remain enclosed by walls of formal and informal regulation that make large-scale investments very difficult or impossible. Access to these service markets should be a priority of Australian trade diplomacy with China and should eventually take precedence over the traditional objective of exporting commodities and manufactured goods.

In principle, China has indicated willingness to open its service sectors to wider foreign competition, through initiatives such as the Shanghai Free Trade Zone (FTZ) and the 'negative list' approach taken in its negotiation of bilateral investment treaties (BITs) with the United States and the European Union, in which all sectors are considered free for FDI except those on an itemised list. In practice, however, progress from rhetoric to reality has been glacial. The

Shanghai FTZ was touted as the leading edge of reform when it opened in 2013, but has achieved no material opening in any major service industry. BIT negotiations are nowhere near completion, in large measure because China's 'negative list' remains far too long to satisfy its counterparts.

There is no easy way out of this quandary and Australia, as a relatively small country, has little leverage. It would certainly be inadvisable for Australia to advance far down the road of a BIT with China until the larger and more powerful United States and European Union have established a high standard for such agreements. In this regard, completion of the Trans-Pacific Partnership – now rejected by the Trump administration – would have been quite important, since it would have established new rules of openness on services trade among member countries, and effectively demarcated the standard that China needs to meet in its own investment agreements.

Finally, although progress on gaining market access in China may be frustratingly slow, it would be wise to resist the temptation to impose some sort of reciprocity standard, under which Chinese firms are barred from investing in sectors that Australian firms are prohibited from entering in China. For one thing, such a measure would be self-defeating, since the vast majority of FDI projects produce benefits such as job creation. And in any case, it would be impossible to design such rules so that they passed any elementary test of fairness. If anything, more needs to be done to temper unease at home over a more visible Chinese investment presence in Australia.

4.

THE SOFT SIDE OF CHINESE POWER
Projecting influence abroad

Telling China's story

China evokes many positive images and much admiration around the globe. Its rich civilisation, cultural achievements and culinary delights are the subjects of great fascination and appreciation. Interest in the study of the Chinese language is growing internationally, recognised as a critically important entry point to understand China's remarkable past and present.

China's economic success has been the envy of the world for a generation and a much-appreciated engine of growth for the global economy. The 2008 Beijing Olympic Games and the Shanghai Expo in 2010 were widely acclaimed as world-class achievements and a glimpse of China's enormous potential. The Pudong skyline in Shanghai, high-speed railway lines across the mountains to Tibet, and the 'Bird's Nest' Olympic stadium in Beijing are just a few of the images that capture our imagination and convey the ingenuity of the Chinese people.

Chinese technology and commercial brands cater to happy customers the world over. Alibaba – the world's largest online shopping company, which recently overtook Walmart as the world's largest retailer – is going global. Its new presence in Australia will make it easier for Australians to access its products; its Alipay system will facilitate mainland Chinese consumers' access to Australian e-commerce sites. Other Chinese companies – including Lenovo, Haier, Huawei, WeChat and UnionPay, to name a few – are helping people to lead more productive, convenient and connected lives all over the world.

Chinese business figures, performers and other celebrities have become household names and garnered fans worldwide. Alibaba founder Jack Ma, basketball star Yao Ming and pianist Lang Lang are among the growing number of Chinese cultural ambassadors who represent the acumen, hard work and appeal of today's China.

In 2013, their first full year in office, Chinese President Xi Jinping and Premier Li Keqiang travelled the world – to Europe, Africa, Oceania, South America, and Central, South and South-East Asia – in an extensive charm offensive, promoting a positive image of China and its new leadership. In Australia, the visit of Xi and his wife Peng Liyuan to Tasmania in November 2014 – the first ever by an incumbent state leader – generated enormous goodwill on the island, which resonates to this day.

Chinese perspectives and images will increasingly emanate from Hollywood as well. Chinese billionaire Wang Jianlin, founder of Dalian Wanda Group, bought the Hollywood studio Legendary Entertainment in 2016. Wanda was already the world's largest operator of movie theatres; the AMC cinema chain is part of its portfolio. In the same year, Steven Spielberg's Amblin Partners and Jack Ma's

Alibaba Pictures Group announced a partnership to facilitate the distribution of Amblin's films in China and help Alibaba gain a foothold in Hollywood's production and distribution business.

Even the People's Liberation Army is working to improve China's image abroad. The *Peace Ark* is the PLA Navy's state-of-the-art hospital ship. Launched in 2007, the *Peace Ark* has sailed around the world providing medical treatment in such places as Africa, the South Pacific and the Caribbean, and assisting in the international response to disasters such as Typhoon Haiyan, which hit the Philippines in 2013. In October 2015, the *Peace Ark* made a goodwill visit to Australia, spending nearly a week in Brisbane. Chinese peacekeepers, operating under the United Nations flag, provide security, medical teams and construction services for people in many of the world's most difficult trouble spots.

But not all aspects of China's image get such favourable reviews. In late July and early August 2016 an extraordinary publicity film played repeatedly on the giant video screen on the north side of New York's iconic Times Square. Complete with catchy pop music, talking heads and picturesque maritime scenes, the video spells out China's historical claims to the islands of the South China Sea and rejects the 'illegal South China Sea arbitration', the international court which only weeks earlier had ruled against most of China's claims in those waters. The three-minute video, paid for by the Chinese government, played 120 times a day for several weeks and was seen by tens of thousands of people. Clearly this was an attempt by the PRC to persuade international opinion to take China's point of view on a highly controversial question.

All of these examples could be considered Chinese soft power at work. As a concept, soft power is difficult to define and means many things to many people. Harvard professor Joseph Nye describes it as the ability to gain preferred outcomes through attraction and persuasion, rather than through force, threats or payments. Non-coercive in nature, soft power often arises not from government policy, but rather from a society's culture, values and image. Some definitions of soft power include efforts to influence public opinion through such channels as political lobbying and media campaigns.

China's government has increasingly turned to soft power to convey positive messages about the PRC, to defend the legitimacy of the Party, and to persuade foreign audiences to accept PRC positions and policies.

This chapter will look more closely at these PRC government efforts to project a positive image and greater influence around the world, with a particular focus on Australia. Many of the positive instances of Chinese soft power noted above do not emerge from the Chinese government. On the contrary, as we will see, the Party faces big challenges in this space.

Machinery and motivations

In seeking to portray a more positive image overseas, the PRC is no different from most other countries. This is the primary task of public diplomacy for virtually every nation. But *how* and *why* China does this is different from most other countries. The Party has from its earliest days taken very seriously the need to craft and control its external messaging or propaganda. The most important Party organ concerned with external messaging, the Propaganda Department, was established in 1921, the year the Party was founded, and drew inspiration from Leninist and other totalitarian systems' use of propaganda as a principal means to assert and maintain CPC authority. Past and current chiefs of the Propaganda Department, typically members of the Politburo, are among the top twenty-five most powerful people in China. Propaganda work is so important that its political oversight is traditionally assigned to one of the members of the Politburo Standing Committee.

The Propaganda Department has a vast remit in overseeing, controlling and censoring how the Party and the Chinese state are portrayed and promoted, both at home and abroad, including through the internet and social media in China, Chinese state-owned media, the Chinese film and publishing industries, cultural exhibitions, education, research and teaching agendas, and through the foreign-relations arms of Chinese national, provincial and municipal government agencies. When Facebook founder Mark Zuckerberg travelled to China in 2016 in the hope of having his social media platform reinstated in the country, he sought and was granted a rare meeting with China's propaganda chief, Liu Yunshan.

So, while China's foreign activities in image-burnishing and opinion-shaping are ostensibly undertaken by organs of the state such as the State Council Information Office, the Xinhua News Agency and Chinese embassies, in fact they are all closely overseen and guided by the Propaganda Department, or, such as in the case of Xinhua, are central organs of the Party itself. Much as China's internal propaganda work aims to legitimise CPC rule in China, so too its external propaganda work abroad aims to do the same.

Given this system, soft power outreach by the Chinese government is tightly controlled as to tone and content. Foreigners on the receiving end of official Chinese image projection – whether from internet sites, social media platforms, broadcasters, press conferences, films or cultural events – will find very little variance, if any, in the messaging from the Chinese government on sensitive issues. The Party's propaganda system is a powerful, generously resourced and well-tuned apparatus at home and increasingly abroad.

Interestingly, the Propaganda Department underwent its own process of image softening as China emerged more prominently on the international stage. In 1998, the department changed its official English name from Propaganda Department to Publicity Department, in recognition of the negative connotation 'propaganda' has in English. However, that image adjustment has not worked out as planned: even two decades later, the new name has not caught on in foreign circles.

While the CPC Propaganda Department is at the top of a hierarchy concerned with projecting China's image and influence abroad through soft power means, the department itself is a relatively secretive and low-profile organisation. You will search in vain to find a website for it. The closest you will get is the website China.org.cn. Operated by the State Council Information Office (which also serves as the Foreign Propaganda Office of the CPC Propaganda Department), this website offers a wide range of official content including government position papers, current events reporting, and basic information on Chinese history, politics, economics and culture.

There are dozens and dozens of other soft power channels through which Chinese authorities aim to improve the country's image and influence in other countries. These include English-language media such as the *China Daily*, the *Global Times* and *Beijing Review*, as well as the websites and foreign market programming of China Radio International (CRI) and China Central Television (CCTV). A recent visit to the CCTV website provided extensive print and video content in English and many other languages, covering topics such as entertainment, sport, money and living, and even including links to 'PandaCams' to watch the adorable creatures live. But the site also prominently features links to editorials and analysis arguing for China's 'undeniable' right to claims in the South China Sea.

In addition to English and other foreign-language media outlets, Chinese-language media is also increasingly targeting Chinese speakers living as citizens or residents in countries outside of China. In Australia, for example, Wanning Sun of the University of Technology Sydney counts no fewer than fifty-nine different Chinese-language print publications in circulation, with most of them closely connected to state-owned media groups in China.[1]

Beyond the media, the PRC looks to exercise its soft power through other means. For example, Confucius Institutes and Confucius Classrooms, now at over 1400 universities and schools worldwide, deliver officially sanctioned learning of Chinese language, history and culture – there were fourteen Confucius Institutes and sixty Confucius Classrooms in Australia in 2015.[2] As detailed below, people of Chinese descent living abroad – called 'overseas Chinese' by the PRC government – are also targets of Chinese official messaging and soft power campaigning.

With the phenomenal increase in the number of wealthy individuals in China – the country now has at least 400 US-dollar billionaires, according to Forbes[3] – expect more Chinese philanthropy to extend overseas and with it an expectation by the Chinese government that it promote 'correct' images and understandings of China. However, it is not certain that the next generation of Chinese philanthropists – especially those who are permanent residents of countries like Australia – will acquiesce to CPC preferences and pressures in the manner that some older-generation Chinese do. Despite the ardent efforts of the Propaganda Department, the Chinese millennial generation has a mind of its own.

What is motivating the Chinese government to step up its efforts in public diplomacy, cultural outreach and opinion-shaping abroad? One simple reason is because it can. With its spectacular economic growth, China has greater and greater resources to invest in soft power. With the explosion in digital technologies over the past two decades and the globalisation of news and information, Beijing has been able to take advantage of these platforms to get its message to an expanding overseas audience. The burgeoning population of Chinese abroad – as students, workers, businesspeople, tourists and permanent émigrés – has also opened new opportunities for Beijing's soft power messaging.

In addition, as China's international profile has grown, so too has the need for the Chinese government to get out in front and shape that profile in a way that is more advantageous to Chinese interests and that assuages concerns about China's rise. Chinese leaders recognise that China's rapidly growing power and influence have created a lot of unease in many parts of the world; they also would know – although not readily admit out loud – that the Party and its authoritarian rule have serious image problems, especially in more open and democratic parts of the world. For China to advance its interests more effectively, it needs to push back against those concerns by conveying a positive, benign and peaceful image.

From the viewpoint of Chinese leaders, the political and economic model of one-party rule and rapid modernisation is an attractive success story, worthy of proud display and emulation by others around the world. As Fu Ying, former Chinese ambassador to Australia, wrote in 2016:

> [I]t's imperative that we make ourselves better understood by the rest of the world … We in China must improve our ideas and ways of thinking faster and form a broader international vision, with more effective modes of expression and behavior. In this way, the rest of the world will be able to better appreciate our culture and the reasons why we talk and act the way we do.[4]

Or, as Xi Jinping has put it, 'We should increase China's soft power, give a good Chinese narrative and better communicate China's message to the world.'

Perhaps most importantly, the constant need to put forth carefully crafted, positive external messaging has been ingrained in the political DNA of the Party for nearly 100 years. But the official Chinese soft power effort has an in-built liability: it is primarily and ultimately about promoting and sustaining the Party itself.

As David Shambaugh shows in his work *China Goes Global: The Partial Power*, advocates for Chinese soft power recognise this liability and urge that the country's soft power messaging abroad focus on more 'acceptable' elements of China's image: its ancient history, its recent economic success and its peaceful traditions. But that pathway is also strewn with complications and contradictions.

Chinese media presence in Australia and around the world

In May 2016, Liu Qibao, director of the CPC Propaganda Department, arrived in Sydney to take part in signing several agreements between

Chinese and Australian media outlets. On the Chinese side were arrayed some of the powerhouses of PRC state-run media: Xinhua, *China Daily*, CRI, *People's Daily Online* and Qingdao Publishing Group. The Australian organisations were Fairfax Media, Sky News Australia, Global China-Australia Media Group, Weldon International, and the Australia-China Relations Institute (ACRI) of the University of Technology Sydney.

Under the arrangement with Fairfax, the *Sydney Morning Herald*, the *Age* and the *Australian Financial Review* agreed to distribute within their regular paper a monthly supplement called 'China Watch', published by the *China Daily* – the English-language mouth-piece of the Party. That agreement, along with the others signed that day, raises many questions. Why were Australian media and academic organisations willing to publish content that conforms to the views of the CPC Propaganda Department? What role is Chinese media playing globally, and in Australian society in particular? Does Chinese media have an unwelcome influence in national debates?

Australians are not alone in asking these questions. Over the past decade, China's major media groups have all launched expansive global initiatives intended to generate greater market share and profits while also burnishing China's image abroad.

Xinhua, China's official state news agency, now has some 170 foreign bureaus and in 2010 established a twenty-four-hour news channel in English known as CNC World, which broadcasts around the world via satellite, cable and online channels. Similarly, CCTV acquired studio and production facilities in Washington, D.C. and Nairobi, Kenya in 2012 with the aim of producing content from the Americas and Africa and broadcasting into these markets and elsewhere around the world in support of CCTV programming. CCTV

America employs more than 160 people and claims that CCTV English-language content reaches 30 million households in the United States through cable and satellite.

CRI broadcasts in more than sixty languages, has some seventy overseas affiliate radio stations and eighteen online radio programs; its English-language programming alone broadcasts more than 600 hours of news, information and entertainment around the world every day. A Reuters investigation in 2015 identified CRI as the primary backer of at least thirty-three radio stations in North America, Europe and the Asia-Pacific, all providing Chinese state-sanctioned programming in Chinese and local languages. In Australia, those CRI-affiliated stations are 1341 AM (Melbourne), 88.0 FM (Canberra), 104.9 FM (Perth) and 90.5 FM (Perth). CRI also leases airtime from radio stations around the world to broadcast news and other programming, which can be very appealing to struggling community radio and smaller-market stations.

These ambitious initiatives are driven by an official Chinese view that the global media – and hence global culture – are dominated by a 'Western' perspective. In this view, if the Chinese Party and state are to succeed in projecting a more positive image of China, they need to compete in the international media marketplace and get the attention of more readers, viewers and listeners.

As Xi said in 2016, the Party and Chinese media 'must strengthen the building of our international communication capacity, increasing our international discourse power and focussing the proper telling of China's story ... working to build flagship external propaganda media that have rather strong reputations internationally'.[5]

One of the most important developments for the growth in Chinese state media has been the boom in digital dissemination technologies. Chinese state media has moved well beyond traditional print and broadcast platforms and actively employs online and mobile channels to convey news, information and other content to hundreds of millions of users worldwide. In Australia, there are some 1.2 million accounts on WeChat, the instant messaging service popular with Chinese users, which is widely used to repost content to users' networks, further extending the reach of Chinese media.

Wanning Sun points out that relatively new social media platforms – such as WeChat, Weibo and Tencent QQ – are increasingly important channels for news and information for Chinese-language users in Australia and around the world. Chinese authorities control and censor the content on these platforms. Professor Sun also flags the emergence of online media outlets operated by Chinese students in Australia which likewise stay well within prescribed boundaries in the information they convey to Chinese-language audiences.

Many analysts have noted that over the past decade or two the tone and substance of Chinese-language media coverage on China in Australia have softened and become more favourable to the PRC.[6] This trend in part reflects a demographic shift. In decades past, Chinese-language media in Australia catered principally to an audience that would tend to have a less favourable view of the PRC: those who fled mainland China in the 1950s and 1960s, persons from Hong Kong or Taiwan, and those from the 'Tiananmen generation' who left China following the violent suppression of protesters in Beijing and other Chinese cities in 1989.

In contrast, today's Australian Chinese media largely targets much more recent arrivals from the PRC, many of whom retain positive connections with China. They would include many of the

150,000 Chinese students in Australia, the more than 1 million Chinese tourists coming each year, and many of the younger Australians who were born in mainland China. The nature of Chinese media in Australia today reflects this demographic shift: according to a report in the *Sydney Morning Herald*, about 95 per cent of the Chinese-language newspapers in Australia are controlled by PRC state-owned media companies.

A good example is found in the Sydney-based Chinese-language *Australian New Express Daily*, which is owned by Chinese real estate tycoon Chau Chak Wing, owner of Kingold Group and a high-profile political donor and philanthropist in Australia. Dr Chau, who is controlling owner of Guangzhou's *New Express Daily*, is also a member of the Guangdong province Chinese People's Political Consultative Conference, a CPC-controlled advisory body. In a 2009 interview with the *Age,* Chau proudly claimed that the Chinese government 'found this newspaper very commendable because we never have any negative reporting'. His Sydney newspaper, edited by his Australian-educated daughter Winky Chau, runs on similar principles, avoiding critical commentary on China.

Hollywood executives have come to understand the power of the Chinese market: if they expect their blockbusters to play on silver screens across China – soon to be the biggest market for movies in the world – they need to soften how the PRC and Chinese are portrayed. It appears that traditional Australian media outlets are following suit. Fairfax correspondent Philip Wen described the decision to publish the 'China Watch' supplement as a matter of 'compelling commercial opportunities'.[7] Fairfax is not alone in this decision. Other papers, such as the *Washington Post* and New Zealand's *Dominion Post* made similar deals with the *China Daily*.

More problematic are the attempts by Australian government-backed media groups to deliver content to Chinese audiences in China. The Australian Broadcasting Corporation (ABC) Chinese-language edition of its *Australia Plus* website exemplifies the potential pitfalls of these kinds of partnerships. Launched in China in 2015, *Australia Plus* aims to share 'stories that reveal the culture, life and society of Australia to inform, inspire and include the diverse audiences of Australia and our region'. However, to deliver this content in Chinese and unblocked by the Great Firewall of China, the ABC contracted with a state-owned media group to translate and post its content on the website.

Not long after, Australian academic John Fitzgerald revealed that this content was entirely devoid of any stories even vaguely critical of China.[8] Investigating the situation in May 2016, the ABC program *Media Watch* found that content had been removed from the Chinese-translated versions of articles written for the ABC Online regarding the South China Sea. Reporting on the discussions about human rights between Prime Minister Malcolm Turnbull and President Xi were removed from the Chinese version, as were mentions about CPC control over Chinese courts. An ABC spokesperson denied that its Chinese partners had any scope to edit or change politically sensitive news reporting and put it down to 'failures in our editorial processes'.[9]

In the wake of these controversies, the ABC has redirected funding to develop its own Chinese-language web content from a .au portal, which will provide a full news service in Mandarin. While this content may be blocked in China, it nevertheless can reach other Chinese-language consumers in Australia and around the world, and do so uncensored. This dual strategy of delivering less-sensitive content inside China while also disseminating a full news service in Mandarin outside of China is similar to what other national broadcasters, such as the BBC, are doing.

In another example, Foxtel, the Australian media firm co-owned by News Corp and Telstra, agreed to broadcast a documentary produced by CCTV and an Australian partner, WildBear Entertainment, which depicts a PRC-approved version of China's 'War of Resistance against Japanese Aggression' during World War II and how it led to the establishment of the PRC in 1949. Partnerships with Chinese media groups even extend to markets in the United States, Europe and Australia which increasingly utilise Chinese state-approved content off the shelf as a cost-effective way to fill the gaps in programming they cannot afford to fill themselves.

In some cases, the Chinese state overtly intervenes in the marketplace to prevent critical Chinese-language media from appearing in Australia. The *Sydney Morning Herald* reported in mid-2016 that the PRC Consulate in Sydney contacted the Sofitel Wentworth Hotel in Sydney and prevailed upon the management to remove an independent Chinese-language newspaper from its lobby. That newspaper had previously published reporting critical of the Chinese government. The same article notes that Chinese government authorities have pressured Chinese companies to only place advertising in PRC-backed Chinese-language media in Australia.

As a result of these trends, according to Professor Sun, there is a 'discernible shift in Chinese language migrant media from a mostly critical to a mostly supportive stance in their coverage of China, the Chinese government, and issues and topics that are considered to be politically sensitive in China'. This trend looks likely to increase as the technologies allow, as traditional media seek new streams of investment and advertising revenue, and as the overseas community from the PRC continues to grow around the world.

Overseas Chinese communities

The more than 50 million ethnic Chinese living outside of China form the world's largest diaspora. In the 2011 Australian census, Chinese ancestry either alone or with another ancestry was claimed by over 866,000 individuals. Today that number would be more than 1 million. According to the Australian Bureau of Statistics, as of 2015, approximately 482,000 of them, or 2 per cent of the Australian population, were born in mainland China. That makes mainland China the third-largest foreign source of Australian residents after the United Kingdom and New Zealand.

As James To, a researcher in New Zealand, thoroughly documents in his book *Qiaowu: Extra-Territorial Policies for the Overseas Chinese*, the Party has long sought to engage and influence this community in order to improve China's foreign image and to advance Chinese policy preferences. The channels of influence are palpably evident. As noted above, the PRC has extensive influence over the content of most Chinese-language media in Australia. In addition, PRC officials enlist ethnic Chinese businesspeople to causes serving China's interests. For example, in early 2016, a number of Australian-Chinese business leaders called upon Prime Minister Turnbull to avoid raising the South China Sea when he travelled to China in April that year.[10] PRC officials conduct surveillance of and at times threaten Chinese international students in Australia through PRC-controlled student organisations and attempt to pressure and muzzle ethnic Chinese critical of the PRC.[11] Top Chinese leaders have explicitly called on all ethnic Chinese overseas, without distinguishing between PRC and foreign citizens, 'to unite as many people as possible to propel China's reform, opening up and modernization drive, and to rally them behind President Xi Jinping's call to achieve the Chinese dream'.[12]

But such efforts have always been a thorny problem for Beijing. In the 1950s and 1960s, owing to a mix of racial, political and ideological fears, Chinese abroad were often vilified as fifth-column supporters of Communist China. This problem was particularly acute in parts of South-East Asia. Hence, the Party had to engage cautiously with overseas Chinese to avoid setting off an anti-China backlash. To this day, Chinese authorities still risk the same accusations, especially as the number of PRC nationals and émigrés around the world continues to grow.

In the early decades of the PRC, Beijing's cultivation of the Chinese diaspora was an important element in its contentious diplomatic struggle with the Republic of China (Taiwan). With China's post-1978 emergence on the world stage and Taiwan's steady marginalisation – today fewer than twenty governments around the world have official diplomatic relations with Taiwan – this part of Beijing's overseas Chinese strategy has become less critical.

The effort to engage and influence Chinese overseas sits uncomfortably with Beijing's professed opposition to interference in the internal affairs of other states. Nevertheless, the engagement and mobilisation of overseas Chinese are important elements in Beijing's foreign policy strategy overall and in its soft power in particular. Through messaging that emphasises Chinese ethnic affinity, cultural longevity, historical achievements and pride in the country's re-emergence as a great power, Chinese abroad can be attracted to express support for the Chinese leadership, their policy preferences and their ambitions.

The organisation ultimately responsible for China's diaspora strategy and diplomacy is the CPC's United Front Work Department. Its goals and policies are then implemented across the Chinese government with the oversight of the State Council Overseas Chinese Affairs Office. The United Front Work Department traces its origins to the earliest days of the Party when it formed a 'united front' with the Kuomintang (KMT), or Nationalist Party, in the 1920s to overthrow the regime then in power in China; a second CPC–KMT united front was established in the late 1930s to defeat the Japanese occupying China. 'United front' has since come to mean identifying and linking up with non-CPC entities and individuals to support the leadership and objectives of the Party.

In ways similar to China's media propaganda work, contemporary efforts to engage and influence individuals of Chinese descent abroad have likewise deployed new technologies and sought new opportunities in the growing number of PRC-born Chinese living around the world. Analysts of the diaspora differentiate between the 'old' and 'new' generations of overseas Chinese. Among the older cohort are those who fled the PRC or hailed originally from Hong Kong or Taiwan, and have a more jaundiced view of the Party and mainland China. As To explains in his book *Qiaowu*, this older community of overseas Chinese was often characterised as 'the three knives': labourers working as market gardeners, restauranteurs, or cobblers and tailors, who made their living with a blade.

The current generation of Chinese abroad is increasingly better-educated, and it includes more wealthy PRC businesspeople, investors, entrepreneurs, students and tourists. Such PRC-born elites in foreign societies are a particularly important channel for the PRC's soft power activities, especially as these elites become more numerous, globalised and mobile. Many of these individuals would retain professional and personal connections with the PRC, have positions of leadership and influence within their own communities, and, importantly, hold a more favourable and patriotic view towards the PRC and the Chinese leadership.

Leaders and rising stars within this newer generation are the subjects of cultivation by Chinese authorities.[13] They are able to avail themselves of powerful connections back in China and are invited to take part in conferences, professional development and networking opportunities in China, all with the watchful guidance and support of the Party. Chinese officials abroad encourage these new migrants to form professional, social and philanthropic associations among their fellow Chinese and help build a stronger sense of 'Chinese-ness', support the PRC leadership and policies, strengthen the political clout of ethnic Chinese, and reduce opposition towards China within the wider society of the host country. It must be said that not all newer-generation Chinese-Australians or permanent residents look favourably upon the PRC. Many are in Australia precisely because they abhor the political system of the PRC. Attempts by Chinese authorities to cultivate positive images of the PRC fall on deaf ears among many of these recent arrivals.

There are hundreds of student, business and community associations serving the Chinese diaspora in Australia.[14] The membership numbers in most are tiny and they are apolitical in nature. Many promote links with Chinese culture among Chinese-Australians, raise money for charity work and disaster relief efforts in China, and provide support for newer arrivals in Australia. Some of these groups are mobilised by the PRC diplomatic mission to ensure enthusiastic welcomes for visiting Chinese dignitaries. Some of the larger, better-funded and more active organisations with close ties to the PRC include the Australian Council for the Promotion of Peaceful Reunification of China and the Australia China Economics, Trade and Culture Association.

Chinese students abroad

Of some 800,000 PRC students studying abroad worldwide, nearly one-fifth – approximately 150,000 – are in Australia. They are a critically important group for China's official efforts to engage and influence overseas Chinese diaspora communities. They are particularly important as they represent China's best and brightest and will, for the most part, return home to contribute to China's development. They also have the opportunity to see China from the outside, with access to news and information critical of the PRC, and are exposed to Western ideas and values – all of which could be problematic for Chinese leaders down the road.

The Chinese government stepped up its efforts to influence PRC students following the crackdown on the largely student-led 1989 Tiananmen protests. With many Western governments allowing overseas Chinese students to stay and seek residency in the wake of the crisis, Beijing recognised that overseas students could become a serious problem. Starting from the 1990s, the Chinese government launched a major campaign to win back the loyalty of Chinese students around the world. As memories of the Tiananmen massacre fade – the vast majority of Chinese studying abroad today were born well after 1989 – this process has become easier.

Much of this work is carried out by Chinese diplomatic representatives based at PRC embassies and consulates abroad. The most direct means by which the PRC government engages and influences Chinese students overseas is through the establishment of Chinese Students and Scholars Association (CSSA) branches on university campuses. Through financial support, social outings and holiday festivals, the embassies and consulates are involved in CSSA activities and ensure they are supportive of the Party and a positive image of China. Working with CSSA members, Chinese diplomats are also able to gather insights and monitor the activities of other organisations and individuals of Chinese descent which could be deemed contrary to PRC interests.

One of the first times Australians came to see this influence in action was in April 2008.[15] This was the year of the Beijing Olympics, and the Chinese propaganda apparatus was in high gear to ensure maximum positive coverage. However, the Olympic torch relay in the month just prior to the Games had met with several embarrassments, especially in London and Paris, where the relay was disrupted by high-profile anti-CPC protests. Fearful that the appearance of the Olympic torch in Canberra would be met with the same kind of opposition, the Chinese diplomatic mission in Australia mobilised thousands of Chinese students to converge on Canberra in support of the relay. Chartered bus transport, accommodation, food, mementos and other incentives were all provided by the Chinese government to guarantee a large crowd in Canberra voicing support for the PRC and the Beijing Olympics.

Similar mobilisation of Chinese students occurs during the overseas visits of major Chinese leaders. The embassy and consulates work to ensure large turnouts of Chinese young people wherever the leader appears. In doing so, the government not only creates the right image. It also hopes to instil a stronger patriotic sense in Chinese youth, as well as to neutralise opposition protests – such as from Falun Gong practitioners or pro-Tibet activists – which often occur during Chinese leaders' visits abroad. In 2014, student organisations used PRC-provided travel stipends to entice Chinese students from across Australia to heed the call of the PRC Embassy in Canberra and its consulates to travel to Brisbane to greet Xi Jinping when he arrived for the G20 summit.

Educational institutions in Australia and elsewhere have felt the presence of Chinese authorities in other ways. Given the importance of Chinese student tuition fees to the balance sheets of universities and schools in Australia, faculty and administrators find themselves under pressure to avoid sensitive discussions in the classroom – about Taiwan or Tibet, for example – or to pass Chinese students in spite of sub-par exam results. In one example, the dean of one of Australia's top business schools was contacted by an official from the local Chinese consul general and asked to ensure certain Chinese students received a diploma because family members had already purchased tickets to attend the graduation ceremony.

Keeping a watchful eye

This kind of official PRC 'assistance' stands in stark contrast to how Chinese authorities treat persons of Chinese descent abroad – even those who are Australian citizens – whom it finds troublesome, whether they are democracy activists, supporters of Tibetan or Uighur rights, Falun Gong practitioners, or students who appear to question the CPC line. In their case, Chinese authorities prefer tactics that discredit, intimidate and silence them.

As documented by former *Sydney Morning Herald* China correspondent John Garnaut, Swinburne University of Technology's John Fitzgerald and others, the Chinese embassy maintains a close watch for dissident behaviour, both among Chinese citizens in Australia – such as students – and Australians of Chinese descent.[16] They do so through the cultivation of informants within the Chinese community who are willing to pass along information about the political, social and religious practices of other Chinese. This is relayed to intelligence authorities in China to assess and, if deemed necessary, act upon.

Writing in the University of Sydney's *Honi Soit* in 2014, Georgia Behrens reported that the greatest concern to Chinese expatriates is:

> the [Chinese] government's tendency to monitor and repri-
> mand its citizens for any involvement in controversial political
> causes ... If you get involved in such an issue ... either you or
> your family residing in China may be invited to 'drink tea' with
> police to discuss your recent activities. 'You'll be asked to visit the
> police station to answer some questions,' one student tells me.
> 'They will hardly ever make proper threats or try to really intimi-
> date you; it will be something more along the lines of, "If you
> keep going down this path, you're going to cause yourself some
> problems, so you should think twice about it next time." That's
> really all that most people need to hear.'[17]

For some Australians, the Chinese government can be far more forceful. In October 2015, the ABC told the story of Michael Li, an Australian-Chinese businessman who claimed Chinese authorities attempted to enlist him as an informant. When Mr Li (who had fled China in 2000 for being a Falun Gong adherent) returned to China in 2004 as an Australian passport holder, he was approached by Chinese security services. In return for reporting on Falun Gong activities in Australia, Mr Li was promised better opportunities for his business in China. When Mr Li refused the offer and returned to Australia, his business interests in China were shut down and he was further pressured by PRC authorities; his brother was arrested in China on tax fraud charges in 2014. Mr Li said of his experience, 'I think [the] Chinese government, their secret police, they have all agents here … It's unbelievable that even [if] I live in Australia, I [am] still under China's police control.'[18]

In another example, University of Sydney Business School tutor Wu Wei chose to resign after it was discovered that he had written derogatory comments about his Chinese students using a pseudonym on the Chinese-language social media site Weibo. Wu used an obscure Chinese word to refer to his Chinese students as 'pigs' and accused them of cheating on their exams by hiring essay writers. (He had earlier gained some notoriety by posting a video of himself burning his Chinese passport and flushing it down a toilet once he had become an Australian citizen, and he had also been vocal in his criticism of the PRC government.)

Chinese students at the university, with the support of the PRC diplomatic mission in Australia, organised an online petition calling for his resignation. In a counterpetition, his supporters stated their concern that 'Mr Wu is becoming a victim of the Chinese government's increasingly intrusive attempts to curb voices of dissent among overseas Chinese. Mr Wu has a long track record of critical comments against the Chinese government, its political system and social affairs on social networks'. Following an investigation by the university, he resigned and apologised for the comments about his students.[19]

It has been uncertain in recent years how the Chinese authorities will treat Australian citizens who were born in the PRC if they were caught up in the Chinese legal system. In several cases since 2009 Chinese authorities have asserted that Australian citizens born in the PRC are considered Chinese nationals.[20] At issue is whether the Chinese government recognises the Australian citizenship of such individuals, thereby allowing them access to Australian government consular services while they are on trial and in detention. The Australia-China consular agreement stipulates that such consular services be made available. However, because PRC authorities have not always complied with this agreement, or have taken issue with whether certain Australian citizens had formally renounced their Chinese citizenship, PRC-born Australian citizens may be at risk of losing access to consular services and protections if they are arrested, tried and imprisoned in China. This uncertainty could be used as a means to intimidate such Australian citizens and casts a shadow of anxiety and doubt across their activities, especially if they are living and working in China.

Political and policy influence

The powerful attraction of the booming China market – and the possibility for Australians to profit from it – has long been an instrument of political influence for the PRC. This rationale seemed to be in play when Australian billionaire Kerry Stokes, who has significant business interests in China, called on the Australian government in 2012 to show greater respect to China. His remarks appear to have been sparked by the Gillard government's 2011 decision to allow US Marines to spend six months a year training with Australian forces outside Darwin. Stokes said, 'We have got to respect China and its position. Human rights have to be seen through China's eyes as well as our eyes,' adding that the Darwin decision had undermined Australia's ties with Beijing.[21]

Stokes is not alone in having a favourable view of China and its interests. Officials in Canberra privately offer many examples of Australian businesspeople appealing to the government to act cautiously towards Beijing – especially on sensitive issues such as the South China Sea or the country's human-rights record – in order to avoid creating any problems in their business dealings with China. Across the region, Chinese leaders work to promote political influence among elites. Sometimes Beijing's leaders offer up carrots. But they are also not shy to wield sticks by threatening to cut off economic benefits – forms of 'economic hard power', which are discussed in the next chapter.

However, the ability of Chinese money to influence Australian politics and policy goes deeper than simply the attraction of the China market. The Sam Dastyari affair is a case in point. The Federal Labor senator and former frontbencher received A$5000 in 2014 from Yuhu Group, a China-based property investment firm, to settle a A$40,000 lawsuit brought against him by an Australian advertising and marketing firm. He also accepted two trips to China as the guest of Chinese institutions, including the International Department of the Party.

In addition to accepting these and other gifts from Chinese companies, Dastyari also spoke publicly in support of Chinese government positions, in direct contravention of his own party's views and those of the Coalition leadership. In mid-2016, at a press conference Dastyari said, 'The South China Sea is China's own affair. On this issue Australia should remain neutral and respect China's decision.' Alongside Dastyari was another Australian citizen, Huang Xiangmo, chairman of the Yuhu Group – who is also president of the Australian Council for the Promotion of Peaceful Reunification of China, a pro-PRC organisation that advocates for Taiwan's reintegration with mainland China. In an earlier Chinese media article, which came to light as part of the affair, Dastyari was quoted as saying that the Australian government must give up its 'hostile stance' in opposing China's imposition of an air defence identification zone around disputed maritime territories.

While Dastyari had done nothing illegal, the incident shed a harsh light on the role of PRC-derived funding in aiming to influence Australian politics and policy. In the wake of these mounting revelations, he resigned from the frontbench in September 2016.

Dastyari is not alone in receiving support from the Yuhu Group. Since 2012, the group has given at least A$360,000 to the Australian Labor Party (ALP). Its recent donations to the New South Wales, Western Australian, Victorian and Queensland branches of the Liberal Party amount to at least A$465,000. In addition, Huang family members and Yuhu Group officials donated A$480,000 to the ALP and the Liberal Party in 2013–2014.[22]

Other China-related donors are also generous supporters of Australian politicians. Chau Chak Wing, a wealthy property developer and owner of Kingold Group and the *Australian New Express Daily*, donated A$1.355 million to Liberal, Labor and National Party coffers. In 2013, Wang Zichun, who listed an address in China's Hebei province on Australian Electoral Commission disclosure documents, donated A$850,000 to the ALP. An ABC report in August 2016 showed that between 2013 and 2015, PRC-linked companies and individuals donated more than A$5.5 million to Liberal and Labor Party accounts, making them the largest foreign-affiliated donors to these two parties.[23]

Huang also donated A$1.8 million to help establish the Australia-China Relations Institute (ACRI) at the University of Technology Sydney, and became the chairman of the institute. Founded in 2014, ACRI is headed by former NSW premier and former foreign minister Bob Carr. The institute's website notes its work is 'based on a positive and optimistic view of Australia–China relations'. In the wake of the Sam Dastyari affair, Huang stepped down as ACRI's chairman, saying he did not want the issue to distract from the 'very good work being done by the Institute'.[24]

In response to the uproar over Chinese donations to Australian politicians, political parties and institutions, Huang wrote an English-language rebuttal which appeared in the Chinese state-run newspaper *Global Times* in August 2016. He described the warnings over such donations as 'groundless' and 'racist', given that donations by individuals of Chinese descent represented a small fraction of all political donations in Australia, and in any event no other ethnic groups – certainly none of European origin – were being accused in the same way. But he acknowledged that 'Chinese donors still need to learn from others about how to participate in politics, how to realize their political appeals by donations, and how to deploy the media to promote their political ideas'. He concluded by saying that Chinese should be 'more confident and active' in Australia's political affairs.

Those such as Chau and Huang are very well connected in both Australia and China and are able to serve as go-betweens for the most senior leaders on both sides. It is clear that this influence is built upon their generous support for philanthropic and political causes in Australia and their continuing loyal connections to the Party.

The PRC government's efforts to influence domestic Australian politics and decision-making – long active but often not visible – has emerged as a contentious and potentially disruptive issue. It is particularly challenging because in many cases it is difficult to confirm the precise actions and effects of such activities which, by their nature, often take place behind closed doors.[25]

PRC-derived funds support Australia's higher education sector and schools, media organisations, China-related research initiatives like the ACRI, and individual politicians and political parties. The flow of money is sometimes accompanied by attempts to determine what is said and not said about China in policy deliberations, public discussions, university teaching and the media, and to help generate uncritical approval of China's government and its domestic and foreign policies among Australians abroad. PRC embassy and consulate representatives have become more open in confronting universities and other institutions to express official displeasure at particular actions or decisions, with the suggestion that the PRC government could take retaliatory action if these are not changed.

The Party's reach

At one level it should be acknowledged that the PRC's image-burnishing in Australia is not altogether dissimilar from the soft power tactics and objectives of other countries. At that level the PRC's efforts can be seen as legitimate and unexceptional.

But at another level, the PRC's attempts to influence views in

Australia are exceptional and lack legitimacy because they are made on behalf of the undemocratic Chinese political system and its methods of citizen control. Some of the interventions in Australia, for example, are directed by the CPC Propaganda Department, whose role in China is to police people's adherence to the views of the Party-State and to enforce 'correct' thinking. It is also exceptional because it brings Australian and Chinese national interests – and values – into direct contention, challenging fundamentals of the Australian political system such as freedom of speech, the press, and enquiry.[26] It also calls for Australian citizens of Chinese descent to be supportive of the PRC and its interests, a possible challenge to Australian sovereignty.

It is critically important for Australians to recognise that relations with the PRC are not simply about straightforward economic transactions. As China rises, it has become increasingly engaged across all aspects of Australian society, and the Party's efforts to influence that engagement have likewise increased. In the vast majority of cases, deepening interaction with China has resulted in enormous benefit for Australia and for Australia–China relations. Both economies have prospered and their free trade agreement provides a foundation for continued economic success. Chinese investment in Australia has expanded. Chinese students bring intellectual capital, research networks and significant financial resources to Australian universities and schools. Australia could be at the beginning of a surge of Chinese tourists. Through the strategic partnership established between the two countries in 2013, Australian leaders enjoy regular access to their counterparts in China.

At the same time, however, Australians need to recognise that there is a deliberate CPC-backed strategy and accompanying action explicitly aimed at influencing opinion inside Australia about China, the Chinese leadership, Chinese policy goals and the Party itself. This effort targets Australian leaders and citizens, as well as those Chinese who are temporary residents here, such as students.

Even a modicum of improved understanding of this point would help inform how best to react to Chinese soft power strategies. For example, according to one source, only a week before the *China Daily*–Fairfax deal for the 'China Watch' insert was completed, a senior Fairfax executive involved in the sign-off was not aware of what the *China Daily* was.

Yet Australians must avoid overly zealous finger-pointing and xenophobic suspicions. Demonising all Chinese would not only be against the Australian values of openness and fairness, but also run the risk of alienating citizens and residents of Chinese descent in Australia and undermine the positive contributions they make to a more globally oriented, productive and diverse society.[27] Australian businesses and universities have made clear that there would be dire consequences in the event that Australia gained an anti-China, anti-immigrant reputation. Chinese trade, investment, workforce talent, student numbers and tourism would decline. Australian political and economic relations with China would surely suffer as a result, as would social cohesion at home.

In addition, Australians should balance their concern about unwelcome PRC projection with the recognition that such efforts face inherent contradictions. While China's rise has surely been impressive, its charm offensive has thus far largely failed to convince its neighbours of its benign intentions. China's relations within the region have not improved significantly over the past decade. In some cases – such as with Japan, South Korea and in the South China Sea – relations have decidedly worsened.

It is also very difficult to assess the precise impact of PRC soft power efforts. For example, the Australian-Chinese community represents an extremely diverse group of individuals, differentiated by their countries of ancestral origin, national affinities, political views, religiosity, and much more. The vast majority will be devoted to their lives as Australians and would be little influenced and probably annoyed by PRC government propaganda. Only a small portion of PRC-born Australians and permanent residents accept at face value attempts by the Chinese government to sell overly rosy and propagandistic messages about their country of birth.

Even more profoundly for Australians, the very reason for concern – that the Chinese political system does not represent Australian democratic values – is the same reason why these soft power efforts in the end cannot fully succeed. Given what the Party stands for, it has a serious uphill battle in attracting Australians to its point of view. Nevertheless, we should expect the Party and the Chinese government to continue to refine their efforts to affect opinion about China, taking advantage of political and economic instruments, new technologies, and the changing demographics and migration patterns of overseas Chinese.

In response, Australian governments, communities and citizens should encourage a transparent national debate about the role of official Chinese influence in Australian society without stirring a populist Sino-phobic response. PRC institutions and citizens that wish to influence Australian politics and society should take part in this debate while providing greater information about their activities, policies and goals.[28]

There are legitimate concerns about PRC influence. But we cannot lose sight of China's impact on Australia's prosperity and the positive contribution Chinese communities make to a thriving multicultural society in Australia. Instead, a balance is needed to more effectively reach out and engage people of Chinese descent in Australia – citizens and visitors alike; deflect and expose unwelcome PRC government influences; and stay true to Australian values, ethics and interests.

Australians should expect tensions to arise from closer relations between two countries with vastly different political and social systems. The PRC's efforts to improve its image and extend its influence in Australia will likely intensify in the years ahead. In response, Australians will need to be better prepared to recognise and address the negative consequences that may come along with it.

5

CHINESE HARD POWER
How will China use its growing strength?

Return of a great power

In September 2015, China staged a massive military parade through the heart of Beijing, on the Avenue of Eternal Peace. The parade was officially intended to commemorate the seventieth anniversary of the end of World War II and China's role in the defeat of Japan. But with martial pageantry, the participation of 12,000 troops, 500 military vehicles, 200 aircraft, and the first-time public display of some of China's most advanced weaponry, the parade also sent an unmistakable message about China's growing military power.

When the Norwegian Nobel Committee awarded Chinese dissident Liu Xiaobo with the Nobel Peace Prize in 2010, the Chinese government sent another unmistakable message: it retaliated by not only putting a freeze on diplomatic relations with Norway, but also shutting down imports of Norwegian salmon and other products and calling off discussions on a bilateral trade agreement. The

Chinese government did so in spite of the fact that the Nobel Committee is not a governmental body.

After several years of intensive effort by the government in Oslo, China and Norway issued a joint statement in December 2016 to mark the full resumption of normalised relations. In the statement, Norway declared that it 'fully respects China's development path and social system' and that it 'attaches high importance to China's core interests and major concerns, will not support actions that undermine them, and will do its best to avoid any future damage to the bilateral relations'. As a Nordic country known for its staunch defence of human rights, the Norwegian government's statement represented a capitulation to China. The Chinese side did not make a reciprocal pledge. Norway's foreign minister said at the time that the normalisation of relations will allow for a resumption of negotiations on a free trade agreement and restore full Norwegian exports to China.[1]

Norway is not the only country to bear the brunt of Beijing's wrath. In response to a visit by the Dalai Lama to Mongolia in late 2016, China temporarily shut down a key border crossing to halt Mongolian mineral shipments, imposed a new tariff on imports from Mongolia, and suspended negotiations over Chinese soft loans to Mongolia. Within one month of the Dalai Lama's visit, the government in Ulaanbaatar expressed regret about its negative impact on China–Mongolia relations, and pledged that it would not allow another visit in the future, in spite of the close historical ties between Tibetan and Mongolian Buddhists. The Chinese foreign ministry spokesman voiced approval, saying, 'We hope that Mongolia will truly learn lessons from this incident, truly respect the core interests of China, honor its promise and make efforts to improve the relations between China and Mongolia.'[2]

Two German scholars have documented the 'Dalai Lama Effect', showing that countries whose top leaders met with the Dalai Lama suffered a two-year reduction in their exports to China.[3]

These are examples of China's growing 'hard power' and its willingness to display and use it. Whereas the 'soft' side of Chinese influence projection – as discussed in Chapter 4 – is often intentionally difficult to discern, China's hard power is far more apparent and deliberately visible. Australia will not be immune from its effects.

One widely cited definition by Harvard professor Joseph Nye states that hard power is 'the ability to use the carrots and sticks of economic and military might to make others follow your will'.[4] Hard power is understood to be largely coercive in nature, seeking to change others' behaviour not through attraction or by example, but rather through pressures, threats and force. And while the term is most closely associated with military power, there are many instruments of economic hard power as well: economic sanctions, boycotts and embargoes, for example. Almost all nations seek to exercise this kind of power in some form, but by definition the most powerful are likely to have the greatest success in doing so.

The remarkably rapid growth in Chinese economic and military strength over the past three decades means that China today can claim a level of hard power capacity it has not enjoyed in over two centuries. There is no doubt this will be employed towards achieving the China Dream of national rejuvenation. The most critical question for Australia and its neighbours is *how* will the

PRC exercise this power? Coercively or cooperatively? Will it be supportive or contrary to Australian interests?

To begin answering these questions we should first look at how China has accumulated this power. From there we can see how and why Beijing has increasingly turned to hard power instruments to pursue its aims, particularly over the past decade. We will also need to consider current and likely future limits to Chinese hard power and then turn to how China might use its hard power in its relations with Australia.

China's pathway to hard power

Growing economic clout

China's burgeoning capacity to exercise economic and military coercion represents one of the fastest transformations of national strength in history. According to the World Bank, Chinese GDP grew from approximately US$177 billion at the outset of the reform era in 1979 to nearly US$11 trillion in 2015 – a spectacular increase of more than 6000 per cent.[5] Using purchasing power terms, China's share of global GDP in 2016 was larger than that of the United States – about 17.5 per cent versus 15.5 per cent – and on a pace to account for fully one-fifth of global GDP by 2022.[6]

China became the world's largest trading nation in 2013 – a first in the world economy since the height of the Qing dynasty of the nineteenth century. Many of the world's major economies – such as Australia, Japan and South Korea – have a high degree of economic dependence on trade with China (see Table 5.1).

Table 5.1: Top 10 trade-dependent economies with China

Country	% of exports by value	% of GDP
Australia	34	6
Taiwan	26	16
South Korea	25	11
Chile	23	8
Japan	19	3
Peru	19	4
Brazil	18	2
Malaysia	12	10
Thailand	12	7
Indonesia	10	2

Data drawn from 'Top 10 China dependent countries', *Forbes*, 26 November 2015, www.forbes.com/sites/kenrapoza/2015/11/26/top-10-china-dependent-countries/#7acc0f4c1f42.

While the pace of China's economic growth is slowing, it remains the largest consumer of iron ore, copper, coal, nickel, zinc, rice, soybeans and many other commodities. As China's middle class grows, its demand for high-quality, diversified and safe dairy and other agricultural products will need to be met. As it is unable to fully meet domestic demand for these commodities, China will need to import much of them, helping ensure continuing trade dependency of many countries on the China market. At the same time, China is the largest producer of certain high-value commodities such as gold bullion and rare earth elements. According to the Stockholm International Peace Research Institute (SIPRI), for the decade 2006 to 2015, China ranked as the world's second-largest importer and fifth-largest exporter of major conventional weapons.

In recent years, China has also become an increasingly powerful source of investment capital around the world. Chinese outward foreign direct investment grew by over 13 per cent in 2015 and reached US$139.5 billion, a six-fold increase over a decade earlier. In 2016, China for the first time became the world's largest 'greenfield' investor – investing in wholly new projects from the ground up – with pledges of just over US$53 billion.[7] Major Chinese investments in 2015 and 2016, such as the ChemChina purchase of the global Swiss agribusiness and biotechnology company Syngenta for over US$43 billion, indicate a growing Chinese interest and capacity to invest in higher-value industries in the West.[8]

At the same time, China has established large lending facilities and infrastructure development initiatives, including the China Development Bank (CDB), the New Development Bank (formerly known as the BRICS Development Bank), the Asian Infrastructure Investment Bank (AIIB), the New Silk Road Fund (NSRF), and the massive One Belt, One Road project. These all point to the country's increasing ability to deploy capital abroad in both developed and developing economies. While still early days, initial estimates suggest that through the AIIB, the CDB and the NSRF, China will pour some US$1 trillion in investment and development assistance into the One Belt, One Road project alone.

Taken together, these data tell us not only that China has become crucially important to the global economy as a whole and to innumerable economic sectors, industries and businesses around the world. These data also show that China is in a far stronger position to exercise its economic clout coercively as an instrument of hard power.

Expanding military might

Alongside its growing economic clout, China's march towards greater military power is also impressive. Since 1990, Chinese military expenditure has expanded nearly tenfold, from just over US$22 billion to approximately US$215 billion in 2015. China today is the second-biggest military spender, behind the United States which in 2015 expended just over US$595 billion. China's military spending now constitutes just over 12 per cent of total global military expenditure and nearly half – about 48 per cent – of military spending in Asia and Oceania. While China's military budget has grown larger and larger, the Chinese government has nevertheless managed to keep its military spending at or below 2 per cent of GDP and around 7 per cent of total government expenditure – these figures are similar to other major powers.[9]

In 2015, Chinese military modernisation took another bold step with the announcement of the most extensive, top-to-bottom reorganisation of the People's Liberation Army in more than thirty years. Among other steps, the restructure empowered the naval, air and strategic missile forces of the PLA and created a new 'strategic support force' to improve the integration of space- and cyber-based technologies across the PLA. Overall, these reforms aim to strengthen the Party's control over the PLA. The reforms also seek to transform the PLA from a bloated and untested military to a more modern and technologically sophisticated force, increasingly capable of projecting power farther and farther from Chinese shores.

China's growing military might is most evident in the areas of air and sea power. China already has the largest air force in Asia and the third-largest globally. The Pentagon estimates that China has about 600 fourth-generation aircraft (roughly similar to the US F-16 or

Russian MiG-29) and that the Chinese air force will likely become a 'majority fourth-generation force' in the next several years.[10] China now operates some seventy submarines and more than seventy principal surface combatants such as missile cruisers, destroyers and frigates. These numbers include the *Liaoning*, China's first aircraft carrier, which entered active service in 2012. More advanced nuclear submarines and a second aircraft carrier are in the pipeline.

The PLA has invested heavily over the past ten to fifteen years in the development and deployment of more lethal missile forces. The PLA Rocket Force currently deploys some 1200 short-range ballistic missiles, mostly opposite Taiwan, as well as hundreds more medium- and intermediate-range ballistic missiles. These are primarily intended for conventional warfare against regional targets, including enemy naval vessels such as aircraft carriers. In addition, China deploys between seventy-five and 100 nuclear-capable intercontinental ballistic missiles, with ranges of up to 13,000 kilometres, meaning they can reach targets in Australia and the United States.

The PRC is also heavily investing in space- and cyber-related capabilities for military purposes. The Chinese 2015 defence white paper makes clear that among the PLA's strategic tasks is the defence of Chinese interests in 'new domains', including in space and the cybersphere. The white paper also states that strategic competition in cyberspace is 'increasingly fiercer' and because 'cyberspace weighs more in military security, China will expedite the development of a cyber force'. With improved and effective cyber capabilities, the PLA will be able to vastly complicate a potential foe's operations and especially those – such as the United States and its allies – which heavily rely on information technology for power projection. The Chinese military will be in a far better position to launch a punishing cyber blow against Taiwan if necessary, either in isolation as a warning or to soften the ground in advance of an invasion of the island.

These expanding resources and ongoing reforms have transformed the PLA into a far more capable and powerful force. And while the PLA still faces many challenges, it has also made important advances which allow China to exercise its military hard power more effectively and deliberately.

Looking abroad, the Chinese military has also significantly stepped up its contributions to international peacekeeping and anti-piracy operations. In 2016, China had more than 2600 troops, police and military experts deployed to ten United Nations peace-keeping operations, mostly in Africa and the Middle East. China's contribution of personnel to UN peacekeeping has been for many years the largest among the five permanent members of the UN Security Council and ranks in the top fifteen of all UN members.

Starting in December 2008, the Chinese navy has continuously rotated a three-ship flotilla to the Gulf of Aden region and off the coast of Somalia, where they protect commercial shipping from piracy. PLA Navy vessels also took part in the escort operations to remove chemical weapons from Syria in 2014 and supported the evacuation of Chinese nationals from war-torn Libya in 2011 and Yemen in 2015. These activities not only contribute to the international community. They also provide the PLA with valuable operational experience in regions far from the Chinese homeland.

Hard power in action

Over most of its three-decade trajectory to great-power status, China has been relatively reluctant to throw its weight around. Instead,

Chinese leaders recognised the need for a generally peaceful external environment so that the country could gain access to vital inputs for its economic growth – markets, capital, raw materials and technology – and stay focused on domestic stability and development. This was the core strategic logic underlying China's 'peaceful rise' and 'peaceful development' concepts from the late 1990s to the late 2000s.

In essence, this approach closely conformed to the well-known axiom coined by Deng Xiaoping that China should be patient and not act threateningly – often translated as 'hide our capabilities and bide our time', or just 'hide and bide' for short.

Of course, this has not always been the case. China was clearly willing to use military force during the Taiwan Strait Crisis of 1995–1996. Alarmed by the moves of Taiwan's then president Lee Teng-hui which appeared to support Taiwan's formal independence from mainland China, the Chinese government undertook an extended campaign of military intimidation. In July and again in August 1995, China conducted missile 'tests', firing volleys of short-range ballistic missiles into waters off the coast of Taiwan. These were followed by major naval drills as well as highly publicised amphibious landing exercises in November, which at the time were some of the largest such exercises ever undertaken by China.

In March the following year, in an effort to influence the Taiwan presidential election, China again fired missiles into the waters off the port cities of Keelung and Kaohsiung – actions that prompted the United States to deploy two aircraft carrier battle groups in the direction of the Taiwan Strait.

A major crisis was averted, but China had made its point through hard power. When an even more pro-independence leader, Chen Shui-bian, was elected Taiwan's president in 2000 and again in 2004, he was unable to gain the support of the United States for his ambition to declare a permanent political separation from China. This was in part because China had made clear it would use force if necessary to prevent that from happening, and Washington did not want a war with China.

China's use of force to threaten Taiwan was an extreme case of blatant hard power. In the decade following that crisis, roughly between 1997 and 2007, China tended to adhere to the 'peaceful rise' and 'peaceful development' concepts. During this period, the Chinese leadership generally sought to ensure a stable environment around its periphery and to reassure neighbours of China's peaceful intentions, all so the Chinese government could focus on critical economic, political and social challenges at home. This also bought time to steadily advance PLA modernisation. The 2002 Chinese defence white paper put it clearly: 'A developing China needs a peaceful international environment and a favorable climate in its periphery.'

However, by the late 2000s and early 2010s, this approach began to change. A number of factors can explain this. First, China's overall security environment has become more difficult. This is especially true as the country becomes ever more dependent on the outside world for vital needs China cannot meet on its own, such as for energy, minerals and food. As China's interests become more global, its security requires stronger capabilities to protect those interests rather than depending on others to do so.

In addition, as noted in Chapter 1, America's 'pivot' towards the Asia-Pacific is largely seen within Chinese strategic circles as a pivot towards – and against – China. Concerns about 'containment' and the belief that the United States ultimately aims to undermine the legitimacy of the Party are never far beneath the surface of Chinese thinking.

Steps taken by the United States to strengthen alliance relations with Japan, including the new 2015 US–Japan defence guidelines, also set off alarm bells in China. For Chinese leaders, the guidelines – which envision closer US–Japan cooperation in missile defence, intelligence sharing, maritime security, weapons development and peacekeeping activities – reflect worrisome changes underway in Japan, especially under Prime Minister Shinzo Abe, to expand Japan's military role in the region.

Other measures taken by the Obama administration to strengthen defence relations with allies and partners in the region – for example, boosting the US military presence in Australia, the Philippines and Singapore, deploying advanced missile defences in South Korea, opening new security ties with Vietnam – are interpreted by Chinese leaders and analysts alike as being deliberately aimed at China. Longtime US military activities in the South China Sea and other locations close to Chinese shores, including surveillance and freedom of navigation operations, are viewed in China as unnecessarily provocative challenges to Chinese sovereignty. In official PRC thinking, it is the United States that is 'militarising' the region, not China.

Chinese analysts also criticise their government's previously acquiescent posture towards the South China Sea. In this view, during the early 2000s PRC leaders did not stand up to actions by other claimants such as Vietnam and the Philippines to take possession and assert sovereignty over islands, shoals and other features in the South China Sea. Chinese leaders today justify their actions in the South China Sea as simply the reassertion of long-standing 'rights' which were wrongfully violated in the past.

There are internal factors at play as well. Under Xi Jinping in particular, more nationalist sentiments have come to the fore within government circles and in broader public opinion, stoked in part by the official narrative of the 'century of humiliation'. Expectations are higher today that the government should push back against foreign transgressions on Chinese interests, especially from the United States and Japan. As noted in Chapter 2, the Chinese government also has rising concerns about domestic socioeconomic challenges and is playing the nationalist card in an effort to distract from and alleviate those pressures through tougher talk and stronger actions abroad. Under these conditions, China's defence and security forces, especially the PLA, are not only able to procure greater resources but also have a stronger voice in internal deliberations and decision-making in responding to external threats.[11]

In many ways, such external and internal pressures are not new. What is new is the increasing ability of China to do something about them.

Wielding economic leverage

Australians should be clear that Chinese leaders are quite willing to exercise economic hard power to prevent or punish actions they deem unacceptable. In 2012, amid the China–Philippine stand-off over Scarborough Shoal, an uninhabited feature in the South China Sea claimed by the Philippines that lies approximately 350 kilometres from Manila and 900 kilometres from the Chinese mainland, China restricted the importation of Philippine bananas. The PRC government officially discouraged Chinese holiday visits to the Philippines, and the Philippine tourism sector took a big hit to its revenues.

In another example, Chinese tourist flows to Taiwan dropped by 33 per cent in 2016 compared with the previous year, following the election of Tsai Ing-wen, head of the independence-leaning Democratic Progressive Party, to the Taiwanese presidency in January that year. Some analysts speculated that the Chinese government discouraged travel to Taiwan as a warning to the new administration in Taipei. About 4 million mainland Chinese tourists travelled to Taiwan in 2015.[12]

Boycotts against foreign products have also been tacitly encouraged by the Chinese government – for example, in 2005 against Japanese goods following the visit of then prime minister Junichiro Koizumi to the controversial Yasukuni Shrine in Tokyo, and the 2008 boycott against the French supermarket chain Carrefour in retaliation for protests in Paris against the Beijing Olympics that year.

One of the best-known cases involved an apparent cut-off in rare earth exports from China to Japan after Japanese authorities arrested a Chinese fishing boat captain for intentionally ramming a Japan Coast Guard vessel in disputed waters in the East China Sea. Subsequent analysis questions whether the reduction in rare earth exports to Japan was actually an intentionally planned punishment in response to the incident.[13] But nonetheless this affair underscored for many how China is increasingly in a position to inflict economic punishment on its trade partners if it wishes. The potential for China to impose such economic costs on Australia rightly weighs heavily on the minds of Australian politicians, policymakers and business leaders.

More broadly, China has been able to leverage its economic power in ways that encourage others to support the Chinese government on key issues of concern to China. One of the most high-profile areas where the PRC has done this in recent years is in relation to the case brought before the Permanent Court of Arbitration in The Hague by the Philippines against China. As it became increasingly clear that the court would rule overwhelmingly in favour of the

Philippines, rejecting the legality of most Chinese claims in the South China Sea – which it did in July 2016 – the Chinese government worked hard to generate public declarations of support for its positions from countries around the world.

According to data compiled by two Chinese professors at Renmin University, at least seventy countries expressed support for some aspect of the Chinese position – either rejecting the jurisdiction of the arbitral court and the validity of the decision or calling on disputants to resolve their differences through dialogue and not in international tribunals.[14] More than fifty of these countries are in Africa and the Middle East, along with other Asian and European countries such as Russia, Serbia, Kazakhstan, Bangladesh, Pakistan, Sri Lanka and Vanuatu. China's economic importance to all of these countries was no doubt a factor when they lined up behind the Chinese government.

The PRC also appeared to wield economic incentives to block the Association of Southeast Asian Nations (ASEAN) from making any reference to the court decision. A gathering of the ASEAN foreign ministers in July 2016 – just two weeks after the ruling was issued – was unable to reach consensus on language making reference to the ruling in favour of the Philippines as part of the joint communiqué following their meeting.

It was Cambodia that objected to such language and assured it would not be a part of the joint communiqué. A week earlier Cambodia had announced a US$600 million development aid package from China. The Chinese foreign ministry officially denied there were any political strings attached to the aid. However, Cambodia – the PRC's closest friend in South-East Asia – is heavily dependent on its economic ties with China and has consistently sided with China's position on the South China Sea.

Chinese state-controlled media outlets are also quite vocal in warning countries to steer clear of policies that the Chinese government deems contrary to Chinese interest or else put their economic relationship with China at risk. When former New Zealand prime minister John Key arrived in China to lead a major trade delegation in April 2016, he was greeted with stern warnings from two of China's leading state-run news organisations, Xinhua and *Global Times,* not to raise the South China Sea issue or risk serious deterioration in the economic, tourism and education relationships between the two countries.

In another example, following Australia's support for the arbitration decision and the Australian government calling on the Chinese government to abide by it, the state-owned *Global Times* issued a stinging rebuke, stating that 'Australia has inked a free trade agreement with China, its biggest trading partner, which makes its move of disturbing the South China Sea waters surprising to many'. The opinion piece continued:

> [Canberra] lauds Sino-Australian relations when China's economic support is needed, but when it needs to please Washington, it demonstrates willingness of doing anything in a show of allegiance … [I]t also intends to suppress China so as to gain a bargaining chip for economic interests. China must take revenge and let it know it's wrong.[15]

More-oblique but still threatening language came from the Chinese government following the Australian government's decision, on national security grounds, to block two Chinese bidders from becoming major investors in Ausgrid, the New South Wales electric power distributor. A spokesperson for the Chinese Ministry of Commerce said at the time, 'This kind of decision is protectionist and seriously impacts the willingness of Chinese companies to invest in Australia.'[16] Australian businesspeople and officials privately note that insinuations by Chinese officials of their ability to inflict economic punishments are not uncommon.

Shows of force

With China's increasing military power, its leaders have shown a greater and greater willingness to employ military and quasi-military means to promote and achieve national interests. China has used military hard power most prominently in and around the disputed waters to China's east and south.

In the East China Sea, both China and Japan lay claim to uninhabited islands that lie between Taiwan and the southern Japanese province of Okinawa. These features are known as the Senkaku Islands in Japan and the Diaoyu Islands in China. They are controlled by Japan and lie in a strategic waterway with plentiful fisheries, potential oil and gas reserves, and heavy international shipping traffic. China claims the islands because they were historically territory belonging to Taiwan, which China maintains is a part of China, and asserts that control over them should have been ceded to China, not Japan, at the end of World War II.

The Japanese government announcement that it would purchase the islands from their private owner in late 2012 – to pre-empt an inflammatory plan by right-wing Tokyo governor Shintaro Ishihara to buy and develop them – set off Chinese diplomatic protests and large-scale anti-Japan demonstrations in Chinese cities. In the PRC's view, the Japanese government's move amounted to a provocative change to the status quo and a greater official assertion of Japanese sovereignty over the islands.

In response, the PRC stepped up the dispatch of fighter jets and patrol aircraft and increased activities of China Coast Guard vessels and commercial ships around the disputed islands. In November 2013, China announced an East China Sea air defence identification zone (ADIZ), requiring foreign aircraft – commercial and military – to identify themselves when flying through the zone. The zone extends to include the disputed islands and overlaps with Japanese and South Korean ADIZs in the East China Sea. In practical terms China's notification requirements have been ignored by many of the military aircraft flying through the ADIZ.

In 2016, China further increased pressure on Japan. According to Japanese reports, Japanese fighters scrambled a record total of 407 times between March and September 2016 in response to Chinese jets approaching Japanese airspace.[17] In August 2016 the Chinese navy staged live-fire exercises involving missile cruisers, submarines and naval aviation in the East China Sea. This was followed by the arrival of a fleet of 230 Chinese commercial fishing ships, escorted by China Coast Guard vessels, to waters around the Senkaku/Diaoyu Islands.

In the South China Sea, China's displays of hard power have been even more assertive. China's maritime claims in the South China Sea are not highly specified, but what is known as the 'nine-dash line' on official Chinese maps encompasses nearly all of the sea. The Chinese government white paper released immediately following the Permanent Court of Arbitration ruling claims that the South China Sea is 'a semi-closed sea' in which 'the activities of the Chinese people ... date back over 2000 years ago'. As such, 'China's sovereignty over Nanhai Zhudao [the South China Sea Islands] and relevant rights and interests in the South China Sea have been established in the long course of history, and are solidly grounded in history and law.' In the words of the white paper, the South China Sea Islands are China's 'inherent territory'.[18] However, at least six other governments also have claims over parts of the South China Sea: Brunei, Indonesia, Malaysia, the Philippines, Taiwan and Vietnam.

While the Chinese government declares its readiness to settle these disputed claims through negotiation, it has nevertheless also built up an expanded military presence in the South China Sea. In 2012, China took control of Scarborough Shoal and until late 2016 ships from the China Coast Guard patrolled the waters around it to forcibly prevent a return of Philippine fishermen and naval vessels. During the visit of Philippine president Rodrigo Duterte to Beijing in October 2016, the two sides reached an agreement allowing Philippine fishermen and patrol vessels to operate in the area. However, China has not ceded claims of sovereignty over Scarborough Shoal and China is able to forcefully refuse Philippine access to the area at any time.

In the most high-profile assertion of its claims in the South China Sea, in a two-year effort starting from 2013, China built seven islands totalling 3200 acres, or about 1300 hectares, in the Spratly Island chain. These new islands, built on top of previously submerged reefs, host a range of facilities such as deep-water wharves, runways, hangars, communications and surveillance systems, and housing, all of which can be used for military purposes. China has also deployed anti-aircraft batteries on Woody Island, the largest of the Paracel Islands, and temporarily stationed artillery on some of the artificial islands in the south of the sea.

In July 2016, just days ahead of the ruling by the Permanent Court of Arbitration, China held its largest live-fire exercise in the

South China Sea to date, carrying out 'air control operations, sea battles and anti-submarine warfare', according to the Chinese defence ministry, and involving ships from all three regional fleet commands of the Chinese navy.

By the end of 2016, China was conducting routine combat patrols with jet fighters and bombers over the South China Sea, and had teamed up with Russia to carry out joint military exercises in the area. In addition, China stepped up its deployment of commercial fishing boats in the South China Sea. These collect intelligence, harass foreign vessels – including run-ins with US Navy ships – and generally advance China's sovereignty claims under the guidance of the PLA Navy.

In all of these activities, the Chinese government is clearly sending a hard power message: that through increased and sustained military and quasi-military activity, including the use of force if necessary, China intends to firmly defend its claims in the South China Sea.

Perhaps most importantly for the future, China is demonstrating increasing capability to deliver on the hard power promise of cyber weapons. The ability to gather information and deliver a debilitating attack on another country has already become an important element of hard power in the twenty-first century. In pursuing these capabilities, China not only gathers useful economic and military secrets through cyber espionage, but also sends a strong deterrent message to would-be adversaries who may be less inclined to confront China for fear of cyber-related attacks on military assets and critical infrastructure.

According to US intelligence sources, Chinese cyber attacks against US government institutions and companies are unprecedented in their frequency and scale. Many of these attacks have been traced to the PLA. The Chinese breach of digital records with the US

Office of Personnel Management (the government's human resources department), announced in June 2015, was one of the largest data heists in US history. It involved the loss of records of more than 21 million Americans, including personal identity information and sensitive data related to individual security clearances, positions within the US government, and other personal and professional background details. In other cases, Chinese hackers have accessed important technical data on US military systems and defence technologies such as the engines used for the F-35 multirole fighter.

The United States is not the only target of China's cyber activities. Other governments around the world have traced cyber attacks and probes to Chinese sources. China is believed to be behind the 2010 theft of the building plans for the new headquarters of the Australian Security Intelligence Organisation. Reports in 2016 revealed that many other sensitive Australian government and corporate computer networks – including those of Austrade, the Defence Science Technology Group, the Bureau of Meteorology, and NewSat Ltd – had been infiltrated by Chinese hackers over the previous five years.[19]

During the 2012 stand-off over Scarborough Shoal, Chinese attacks were launched against the websites of the University of the Philippines and *The Philippine Star* newspaper to display nationalist Chinese messages. A week after the July 2016 Permanent Court of Arbitration ruling, Chinese hackers were able to penetrate the computer systems of Vietnam's two largest airports and broadcast pro-China announcements on their information screens and over their public address systems.

These are a few public examples. Because governments and corporations are often reluctant to reveal when an attack has taken place, or may prefer to keep them secret so that they can monitor and counter the attackers' activities, much malicious Chinese cyber activity goes publicly unreported. Cyber attacks can sometimes be difficult to attribute with specificity.

But it is clear that China increasingly recognises the importance of cyber warfare in all of its dimensions and is rapidly building its capacity to integrate both offensive and defensive cyber weaponry into its hard power arsenal. And it has good reasons to do so. From China's point of view, it is itself the target of cyber intrusions and other electronic surveillance against its military and other sensitive sites. The US government readily admits that it undertakes such intelligence-gathering as a matter of routine. In the event of war with a technologically advanced adversary, the PLA knows that cyber attacks will be part of the fight, so it needs to be prepared to prevent them and deliver counterattacks of its own.

Constraints on Chinese hard power

In addition to recognising China's growing power, it is equally important to consider persistent constraints on that power. Some of these constraints are deeply structural and will be extremely difficult for China to overcome. Some constraints arise as external actors look to counterbalance China's greater assertiveness, and others arise from within China itself.

Structural constraints

Take for example the hard reality of China's geostrategic position – where it sits on a map. China today has the world's longest land borders, extending some 22,150 kilometres. With direct land frontiers with fourteen states, China has the most land neighbours in the world (tied with Russia). China also has maritime borders – often disputed – with several others including South Korea, Japan, Taiwan, Vietnam and the Philippines. China has had or now has territorial and sovereignty disputes with nearly all of them.

Moreover, four of China's land neighbours are nuclear-weapons states: Russia, India, Pakistan and North Korea. If America's forward-deployed nuclear weapons capabilities are included, that number increases to five. In addition, four of China's closest neighbours – South Korea, Japan, the Philippines and Thailand – are treaty allies of the United States.

China's strategic centre of gravity, its developed coastal region, as well as its very high dependence on imports and exports by sea, are vulnerable to being cut off and disrupted. China's ability to project sea power far from its shores must contend with the geographic reality of the first island chain – the islands and archipelagos made up of Japan, Taiwan, the Philippines, Indonesia, Singapore and Malaysia – which stands between China and the more open waters of the Pacific and Indian oceans.

Looking inside China itself, other geographic and demographic realities come to light. For example, only about 11 per cent of China's land is arable, a figure under intensive pressure owing to urbanisation, desertification and other environmental degradation.[20] China's landmass makes it the world's third-largest country in territorial size, slightly larger than the United States. But, remarkably, about half of the Chinese landmass – 49 per cent – is made up of just four regions: Tibet, Xinjiang, Inner Mongolia and Qinghai, traditionally territories of non-Han peoples. Tibet and Xinjiang in particular are home to restive ethnic and religious movements.

As long as leaders in Beijing worry about stability in these regions, they will need to reserve some hard power capabilities to deal with potential unrest and will remain wary of the possibility that forces outside of China may wish to exploit them. Indeed, the Chinese government devotes more spending to maintaining internal security than it does on its traditional military budget.[21]

China's future demographic picture could also place constraints on its comprehensive national strength. China's population is ageing rapidly: over the next twenty-five years the ratio of working-aged people to retirees will rapidly shrink from about six to one today to two to one in 2040. China will grow old before it grows rich.

In short, China faces significant structural challenges of geography and demography, which at a minimum will place considerable constraints on the country's comprehensive national power. In extreme scenarios, these challenges could weaken China and undermine its hard power capabilities over the medium to long term.

Counteractive constraints

But China faces constraints in the near term as well, as external actors look for ways to counteract Chinese assertiveness.

For example, there are many cases where Chinese economic hard power has fallen well short of achieving China's stated aims. North Korea is one such example. There is probably no other country more economically dependent on China than its communist neighbour, North Korea. In 2015, more than 75 per cent of North Korea's exports and imports were with China. Chinese firms are far and away the largest investors in North Korea. China has North Korea's longest and most open land border and is the principal gateway through which goods flow in and out of the country. This dependency has deepened since the late 2000s as other countries, particularly South Korea, have drastically curtailed economic relations with the North, especially with stepped-up United Nations Security Council sanctions following North Korea's continued nuclear and missile testing in defiance of the international community.

In overall compliance with UN sanctions and seeking to moderate the North Korean government's provocative actions, China has applied economic hard power against North Korea. Yet China is reluctant to fully cut off its economic ties with North Korea – and most importantly its supply of energy resources – for fear that it could lead to a chaotic collapse of the country. As a result, China continues to be frustrated by its inability to compel North Korea to halt its nuclear and missile programs, bring about greater stability on the Korean peninsula, or encourage the Kim regime towards Chinese-style economic reforms. So in spite of economic pressure, China has not achieved its aims with North Korea.

Another example of the limits of Chinese economic hard power involves South Korea. South Korea is quite dependent on economic ties with China. Some 26 per cent of South Korean exports and 21 per cent of its imports are with China. About half of South Korean tourist visits come from China. Chinese form the largest group of foreign students in South Korean schools and universities – at many universities Chinese students make up well more than half of the foreign student body. The value of South Korean exports to China, Chinese investment in South Korea, and Chinese tourism in South Korea is equivalent to about 11 per cent of South Korean GDP, making the South Korean economy one of the most China-dependent in Asia.[22]

This dependency was very much at issue as South Korea deliberated whether to deploy an advanced anti-missile system known as Terminal High Altitude Area Defense (THAAD) to protect the country against North Korea's missile arsenal. The Chinese government fiercely objected to the deployment, claiming the system could be used against China. The Chinese ambassador in South Korea stated bilateral ties 'could be destroyed in an instant' and 'could take a long time to recover' if Seoul decided to go forward with the missile shield. In China, public boycotts of South Korean goods were threatened. In spite of this economic intimidation, South Korea nevertheless made the decision in July 2016 to deploy the THAAD system in cooperation with the United States.

China's latest large-scale initiatives to assert greater economic clout, such as the One Belt, One Road initiative, are still in relatively early stages. The grandest ambitions of OBOR will face the same hurdles all infrastructure development programs face in harsh sociopolitical climates as in Central and South-West Asia and Africa. Many sceptics, including some in China, point out that OBOR thus far has been mostly sloganeering and lacks a cohesive strategy. Time will tell, but Australians and other outsiders should be cautious in assuming Chinese leaders will always succeed in achieving their economic ambitions or exercising economic hard power.

China's military hard power also has significant limitations. As noted above, China sits in a complicated and potentially very dangerous neighbourhood. Leaders in Beijing, while more willing in recent years to take military risks, have nonetheless done so in cautious and calculated ways in order to avoid outright conflict with other regional powers, including the United States. Hence, for example, China *could* even more actively militarise the South China Sea, attempt to strictly enforce its ADIZ in the East China Sea, or more openly threaten or even attack foreign navies operating in waters it claims. But it has not done so. Instead, the PRC must limit its hard power tactics below a threshold it calculates will avoid the outbreak of hostilities while still achieving step-by-step progress in asserting its claims.

Beijing's leaders have good reasons for thinking this way. Some of China's principal hard power targets are allies of the United States as well as the United States itself. Pushing too hard against the United States and its allies can be highly risky. The United States remains the world's most formidable military power, and in concert with allies such as Japan and Australia it is even more powerful. The United States has permanent bases in Japan, South Korea and Guam, and extensive military, security and defence technology ties with other key partners such as Australia, Singapore, the Philippines and Taiwan. Moreover, the United States has forged security relationships with others in the region – for example, extending assistance to Indonesia, Malaysia and Vietnam to develop their maritime patrol and surveillance capabilities.

Those in the region who have concerns about Chinese hard power and how China intends to use it have welcomed a strong US regional presence and its closer security engagement with partners across the Asia-Pacific. In the face of growing Chinese military power, many of China's neighbours – both US allies and non-allies alike – have sought ways to counterbalance that power and constrain China's ability to exercise it coercively.

This is especially true of Japan. US–Japan defence relations have grown closer in recent years, in many ways as a response to China's expanding military footprint. In 2014 and again in 2015, in the midst of heightened tensions between China and Japan over the Senkaku/Diaoyu

Islands, then US president Barack Obama made clear that because the islands were administered by Japan, the US defence alliance commitments to Japan would apply to them. These were important statements, in effect underscoring for China that the United States would act to defend Japan if a conflict were to erupt over the islands. Citing an 'increasingly complex security environment' – a reference that no doubt includes China's growing power – the new US–Japan defence guidelines stress the need to activate alliance responses even when Japan is not directly attacked but where its security is otherwise endangered.

Even in the face of growing Chinese assertions of hard power in the East and South China Seas, the United States continues to operate its military vessels and aircraft in these areas to show it does not accept China's expansive claims or its declaration of an ADIZ. As Obama and his leading defence officials repeatedly said, 'We will continue to fly, sail, and operate wherever international law allows.' That policy will likely continue under President Trump.

Lack of experience

China's military hard power faces many external constraints, but it faces internal constraints as well. These largely arise from persistent operational and organisational limitations of the PLA, which are far more important than increased military budgets and advanced hardware in preparing the Chinese military to use force in a modern-age conflict. The PLA fully recognises these constraints and has over the past two decades worked hard to address them, but critical gaps remain.[23]

The PLA's lack of operational experience is just one major example. This has at least three important dimensions. The first is simply the lack of combat experience. The Chinese military last fought a conflict in 1979 when it invaded Vietnam as punishment for Vietnam's invasion of Cambodia the previous year. That intervention was short-lived and, for China, disastrous: some 26,000 were troops killed, tens of thousands more wounded, and the political aim of forcing Vietnam to withdraw from Cambodia was not achieved. Today there would be very few senior officers remaining in the PLA who saw action in that conflict nearly four decades ago; lower down the ranks of officers and soldiers, there would be no one who has fought in a protracted war.

Second, the PLA has scant experience in conducting joint operations. The calamitous incursion into Vietnam in 1979 was conducted by China's land forces, the PLA Ground Force, and did not involve coordination with other services such as the air force or the navy. This raises serious questions about the effectiveness of the PLA as a whole in a modern warfare environment where integrated operations across different elements of the military are critically important.

Third, the PLA of today has no experience in wartime operations in the sea, air, space or cyber domains. Most analysts, including those in the PLA, recognise that China's future threats and possible conflicts will arise offshore in its near seas and will involve operations below, on and over water, as well as in the new domains of space and the cybersphere.

Some of this lack of experience is addressed through more realistic training, the PLA's participation in UN peacekeeping, conducting counter-piracy patrols and escorts in the Gulf of Aden, and exercises and other interactions with foreign militaries, such as with Russia. But while these are no doubt helpful in preparing the PLA for using force in a real-world conflict, they cannot replace the lessons of combat experience.

What next for Chinese hard power?

Looking ahead, how will China use its growing hard power and what are the implications for Australia? To begin, Beijing will increasingly look to exercise its economic hard power in a variety of ways to achieve its overall interests. As discussed in Chapter 3, while the pace of its economy is slowing and facing some difficult headwinds, China will nevertheless remain a powerful economic partner and an attractive market. Even at an annual growth rate of 6.5 per cent, China added more than US$700 billion to its GDP in 2016.

Moreover, in part as a response to those headwinds, the Chinese government is in the early stages of building a global and regional network of economic institutions and initiatives to bolster China's economic clout around the world. By deploying its massive capital reserves abroad, China will further deepen its influence in regional and global economic governance through such initiatives as AIIB and OBOR. China will aim to become a more and more important provider of capital and technology to bilateral partners, especially, but not exclusively, to those in the developing world. Burgeoning demand from Chinese upper and middle classes for foreign consumer goods, international education, real estate investments, and leisure travel will also be an increasingly important factor in bolstering the PRC's economic influence in developed economies and its potential leverage over economic partners.

This presents both opportunities and challenges for Australia. Clearly, Australia's economic relationship with China has flourished. But this flourishing relationship also gives the PRC the increased ability to threaten and use economic coercion in its relations with Australia. Chinese leaders could decide, for example, to discourage Chinese students and tourists from going to Australia in response to

155

an Australian decision the Chinese government sees as contrary to its interests. Though such a step would signal a very harsh new approach for China, it is worth noting that following the election of Donald Trump, China's state-run *Global Times* newspaper warned that the PRC could limit the number of Chinese students in the United States in the event that Washington imposed stiff tariffs on Chinese imports.[24] Australian political leaders and the broader public need to be aware of the pronounced intertwining of security and economic interests with China, the ways in which Chinese leaders can exercise economic hard power against Australia, and the trade-offs and difficult decisions that will ensue.

China's military hard power is growing as are its abilities to threaten Australia and Australian interests. But China is unlikely to launch a war or otherwise militarily attack its neighbours in the foreseeable future. Chinese leaders recognise the country's strengths lie primarily in its economic power. They would also harbour doubts about the PLA's capabilities, all the more so as the military goes through a difficult political and organisational restructuring. Chinese political leaders and military planners still very much wish to avoid an open conflict with the superior forces of the United States and the additional strength it draws from its allies and security partners in the region.

Instead, China will develop and exercise its military hard power in far more sophisticated ways, intended to stay below the threshold of conflict. This will include the continued steady build-up of military capabilities, but with a particular focus on improvements to operate in the maritime, aerospace and cyberspace domains. This will surely include the continued build-up of militarily relevant facilities on Chinese-controlled islands and other features in the

South China Sea. The PLA will intensify training and exercises which also serve to signal readiness and new competences to its neighbours. The Chinese will expand the role and capabilities of 'white hull' China Coast Guard vessels to patrol and monitor disputed areas in China's near seas. These ships can readily monitor and defend most of the maritime areas China currently administers but send a less provocative message than 'grey hull' warships. The PLA will continue its extensive cyber-probing to gather relevant intelligence and uncover the vulnerabilities of potential adversaries. All the while, expect the PLA to expand international peacekeeping, counter-piracy and other cooperative activities with other militaries, including with the Australian Defence Force, as these activities help improve PLA capabilities but also convey a less threatening image of Chinese military might.

As the Chinese military goes down this pathway, it will continue to face the constraints noted earlier – strategically, operationally and organisationally. But in the areas around its immediate periphery – such as in the South China Sea, the Taiwan Strait and the East China Sea – the PLA will steadily build its capacity to threaten, put at risk, and deter foreign militaries operating in these areas. This is especially true for its smaller neighbours such as the Philippines, Malaysia and Taiwan. It will be increasingly true for other more powerful militaries such as Australia, Japan and the United States. In doing so, China does not intend to disrupt commercial shipping in these waterways. Rather, China aims to push the envelope of its military effectiveness outward so it can dissuade and deter foreign militaries from operating with impunity in seas so close to the Chinese mainland. Over the longer term – perhaps in the next five to ten years – this could mean a stand-off with the United States, Australia and others who wish to conduct freedom of navigation and over-flight operations in areas they claim as international waters and airspace, but which China wishes to claim as sovereign territory.

In the near to medium term, however, China will largely pursue a strategic calculation that its regional neighbours overall prefer to have a constructive relationship with China which avoids conflict, even as they will try to counteract Chinese activities which impinge on their most important interests.[25] Even the United States has pursued this delicate balancing act with China, a combination of engaging and hedging, or working for the best while preparing for the worst. So too must Australia. But Canberra's policies of engagement and hedging with China need not follow in lock step with Washington. This is all the more so if US–China relations were to significantly worsen under President Trump.

There is a risk that China will overplay its hard power hand. This is especially true as more nationalistic and even xenophobic messaging comes from the media and other propaganda organs of the Party, pushing both official and public attitudes in more strident directions. This in turn leads subordinate elements of the Party, state and society – government agencies, state-owned enterprises, the PLA and other key actors for China's international relationships – to take up the chorus and assert Chinese interests by lashing out with hard power. That could result in inadvertent military confrontations and clashes in disputed waters between China and other claimants, spiralling into a larger regional conflict. It could also mean a greater willingness in Beijing to impose retaliatory economic punishments in response to perceived offences.

Before the nineteenth CPC National Congress at the end of 2017, it seems unlikely Xi Jinping would encourage actions that could jeopardise a smooth transition to his second term. However, if he is successful in gaining a strong mandate and installing trusted supporters in key positions of power, the world may face an even more confident and risk-taking Chinese leadership in 2018.

Australia should be prepared for these possibilities. On the positive side, Australia has some leverage in dealing with China. For example, as Peter Drysdale and colleagues have pointed out, Australia is China's seventh-largest source of imports, a significant and reliable provider of key economic inputs from iron ore to higher education, and a like-minded partner in support of global and regional economic growth in the G20, the Asia-Pacific Economic Cooperation (APEC) forum and the Regional Comprehensive Economic Partnership (RCEP).[26] That said, like many others in the region, Australia needs to recognise its limited ability *on its own* to shape or deflect China's use of hard power.

In the end, Australia's best strategy for avoiding the potential hazards of Chinese hard power lies in strengthening and diversifying its economic, diplomatic and security engagements not only with the United States but with the full range of global and regional partners. This certainly does not mean shunning or 'containing' China, which in any event is not possible. In fact, Australian strategy must do a better job of engaging China itself, with a far greater understanding of the sources, constraints and likely uses of Chinese hard power in the years ahead.

6.

GETTING IT RIGHT FOR AUSTRALIA

Australia and China have never had such a promising and inter-dependent relationship as today. Chinese tourists are the largest group of visitors from abroad and the biggest foreign spenders in Australia. Up to ninety direct flights arrive in Australia from China every week, with more to come. China is now the largest buyer of Australian wine, surpassing the United States in October 2016. Nearly one-fifth of Chinese students abroad choose Australia as the place to pursue their studies. Fifty-four per cent of Chinese demand for iron ore is met by Australian exports.

But Australians beware. It has not always been this way.

Since the mid-1990s, Australia has twice found itself in the sin bin. In 1996, China froze relations for several months following John Howard's meeting with the Dalai Lama. This was a breaking point after numerous decisions by the Howard government that year which had upset Beijing. China's media reacted ferociously to the meeting, stating that Australian politicians were 'in league with the Devil' and 'unwilling to abandon their evil intentions of interfering in China's internal affairs'.[1] In those days Australia was not dependent on China: exports to China constituted less than 5 per cent of total exports.[2]

Thirteen years later Australia was again out of favour. A former Australian ambassador to Beijing has described 2009 as the '*annus horribilis*'. During this frosty time, Australia under Kevin Rudd's stewardship published a defence white paper identifying China as a potential threat; a Rio Tinto mining executive received a ten-year prison sentence in China; Rudd condemned ongoing repression in a speech to mark the twentieth anniversary of the Tiananmen crisis; and Chinese officials exerted substantial pressure on Australian officials to prevent the visit of a prominent Uighur leader. In contrast to 1996, this time China's displeasure was of greater significance to Australians. By 2009, China had become Australia's largest trading partner, overtaking Japan, largely as a result of soaring demand for iron ore, coal and liquefied natural gas. By 2010, over one-fifth of Australian exports went to China; by 2015 that figure had reached one-third.[3]

To understand how Australia–China ties recovered from these low points requires looking beyond the direct relationship to developments in the Asia-Pacific region, especially China's rise and its effect on US strategy. In particular, Barack Obama's visit to Australia in November 2011 placed Australia squarely in the sights of strategic planners in Beijing. Obama announced that the United States, as a Pacific power, would boost its economic, diplomatic, cultural and defence capabilities across the region. Though Obama did not use the term in his Canberra speech, the US 'pivot' to Asia was elaborated in statements by senior American officials.

The Australian media focused on the announcement that US Marines would henceforth regularly train in Darwin. But in Beijing they also noted both the US–Australia agreement to substantially increase military cooperation and Obama's speech to the parliament. As China's leaders saw it, Obama stood before Australia's political elite and questioned the legitimacy of Communist Party rule in China. His exact words were: 'Other models have been tried and they have failed – fascism and communism, rule by one man and rule by committee. And they failed for the same simple reason. They ignore the ultimate source of power and legitimacy – the will of the people.'[4]

After Obama's visit, influential figures across the Australian political spectrum – including Bob Carr and Malcolm Turnbull – voiced concern over Prime Minister Julia Gillard's unconditional embrace of Obama's rebalancing strategy – the pivot. Former prime ministers, former cabinet ministers, former diplomats, retired military officers and respected foreign-policy commentators went even further and questioned the rationale for the decisions announced during the Obama visit. At the same time, many Australians viewed with concern China's growing power in the region. Gillard steadfastly clung to her position that it was possible for Australia to have an ally in Washington and a friend in Beijing. She repeatedly said that increased US military training on Australian territory posed no threat to China.

All the while, with the help of trusted senior Australian public servants, Gillard was quietly putting in place a significant mechanism to improve the Australia–China relationship. Since the *annus horribilis*, China's regional power and confidence had grown, as had its economic importance to Australia. For this reason, Australia needed a more constructive relationship with China, as well as stronger ties to America. Gillard recognised that Australia's prime minister needed to interact regularly with China's premier to understand and discuss Chinese thinking on not only bilateral but also regional issues.

During her visit to China in April 2013, Gillard and Premier Li Keqiang announced a strategic partnership between the two countries, including an annual leadership dialogue at which the Australian prime minister, foreign minister and treasurer would meet with their Chinese counterparts. Eighteen months later the Abbott government oversaw another milestone, the signing of the China–Australia Free Trade Agreement. Despite five changes of prime minister between 2007 and 2016, the Liberal and Labor parties have by and large supported a policy that seeks a deeper and more fruitful relationship with China.

Following these major breakthroughs, it was clearer than ever that Australia and China share certain fundamental strategic goals, including maintaining a stable and prosperous region. The leadership dialogue powerfully signals a political commitment by both sides to the relationship. The leaders not only discuss common interests, but also have in place mechanisms to discuss the thorny issues that inevitably arise between two countries in an all-encompassing relationship.

Donald Trump's presidency and the uncertainty it injects into the region's future make the annual leadership dialogue between Australia and China more significant than ever. This direct communication channel with China's leaders will be extremely useful to Australia's prime minister and other government ministers at a time when regional developments are unpredictable. Building political trust between Australia and China has never been more important. This regular meeting between leaders is an opportunity to build such trust.

At the same time, Australians should recognise that the relationship is lopsided. Australia needs China more than China needs Australia. This disparity greatly complicates Australia's ability to pursue its interests.

Challenges and changes

Complicated has many meanings. For all its interconnectedness and shared interests, the Australia–China relationship faces many challenges. The 2016 decision by Foreign Minister Julie Bishop to have a new China strategy written was a long-awaited and necessary initiative. Six whole years had elapsed since the previous China strategy. In November 2016 the National Security Committee (NSC) spent an hour discussing the paper. Several of the meeting's participants emphasised that it was unusual – and useful – to spend 'a full hour' discussing Australia's relationship with China in a comprehensive manner. It is surprising that the NSC does not do this more regularly.

Many Australians, including in the government, are concerned about how China will use its growing wealth and power. Chinese officials, in turn, see in Australia an unwise willingness to side with the United States on crucial and sensitive issues. In business, Australian executives have for years complained about unfair practices within China, while of late some Chinese investors feel they have been discriminated against in Australia. The Chinese authorities' crackdown on civil rights and their warnings about the dangers of Western influence inside China arouse concern in Australia. Australian authorities, when pressed, will acknowledge the risks of Chinese government efforts to influence Australian politics and society.

Moreover, the environment in which Australia and China engage one another has changed dramatically. China and Australia are both feeling the pressures of globalisation, which threatens to undermine interdependence. Leaders are tempted to turn inward and adopt protectionist policies. The threat of violent extremism as well as unruly domestic politics have in recent years diverted Australian leaders from focusing on China. Whether that will still be possible in the era of Donald Trump remains to be seen. Domestic debate about the future direction of Australia's alliance with the United States will also shape ties with China.

China has also changed. A mere decade ago, many in the region were hopeful that it would rise peacefully. Today China seems increasingly nationalistic and willing to use hard power to pursue its strategic interests. A decade ago, there was optimism that China's political system was evolving towards greater openness and accountability. Today, under Xi Jinping, the Communist Party has tightened its grip on free expression and seeks to reinvigorate the role of the Party in economic, social, educational and intellectual affairs.

At the same time, the role of the United States in the region is uncertain. Since Trump's victory, doubts have become more persistent than ever as to America's commitment to remain the dominant power in the Asia-Pacific. Some foresee the United States neglecting the region, which would encourage China to assert itself more forcefully. Others predict the United States will become more confrontational by launching a trade war with China, reinterpreting the sensitive 'One China' principle, and strengthening America's military presence in the South China Sea and elsewhere on China's periphery. In either case, Australia's predicament will intensify. How should it balance its relationship with these two major powers, both of which are integral to Australia's prosperity and security?

Many of the challenges in the Australia–China relationship have emerged relatively recently, in just a decade. The Trump presidency may well add another layer of uncertainty and insecurity. Consequently, Australians and their government struggle to keep up. These challenges loom even larger as China's era of phenomenal economic growth comes to an end. During economic good times the problems in the relationship were easier to manage or ignore. No longer.

Looking ahead, there will be many instances when Australia will have to stand up to Chinese pressure and withstand its wrath. At other times Australia will have to accommodate China. This means choosing battles. In times of uncertainty and change, when long-held assumptions are challenged, leaders need to think hard about what really matters, and about core national interests. Above all, Australia must seek to uphold its principles while also maintaining prosperity and security.

Principles

Xi's China Dream does not sit comfortably with Australian dreams and aspirations. Australians will always be uneasy with a one-party authoritarian state. Australian concern about the Party's crack-down on 'hostile international forces' – read, proponents of Western ideals – has intensified under Xi. Chinese authorities explicitly reject these ideals as dangerous, among them such concepts as constitutional democracy, universal values, civil society and press freedom.

The most alarming encroachments on Australian principles are the attempts in Australia by Chinese authorities to undermine academic freedom and integrity, stifle freedom of expression, influence the tone and content of media reporting on China, and shape the views of Australian politicians. All governments conduct outreach activities in other countries to enhance their image and influence. In the case of the PRC, however, these efforts are made on behalf of a one-party state. As China's power grows, Australians should prepare for innumerable attempts at influence-buying through business, political parties, academia, think tanks and the media. As Stephen FitzGerald, Australia's first ambassador to the PRC, has written: 'What is at play here is a soft power offensive with a hard edge.' He also calls it 'Soft Power with Chinese Party-State Characteristics'.[5]

In spite of Australian aversion to such meddling, China's shadow looms large. Too often Australians pre-emptively placate Chinese partners or government officials. Sometimes this takes the form of self-censorship or avoiding sensitive issues altogether. For example, some Australian event organisers fret over an attending Chinese consulate official taking offence and retaliating if critical views of China are aired. Ironically, such behaviour in Australia finds a parallel in the self-censorship and constraint on open discourse among intellectuals in China. Such pre-emptive cave-ins are unhealthy for Australian society.

Despite such reservations, Australia should not shun China. China will remain absolutely central to Australia's economy and security for decades to come. Only through engagement can Australia expect to glean insight into how China works and the aspirations of its leaders. Smart policy choices demand an understanding of Chinese leaders' motives, even if we do not like their system of government.

The mere thought of shunning China is foolhardy. There are roughly 1 million Australians with Chinese ancestry. Close to half a million residents in Australia were born in the PRC. Close to 150,000 PRC nationals are studying in Australia and more than 1 million Chinese tourists visit Australia each year. They are major contributors to Australian prosperity and diversity. This influx has naturally raised concerns about the potential for espionage and other illegal activities, drawing the attention of Australian domestic security services. However, Australians should not succumb to paranoia, or overstate the risks these individuals present. If such assessments become dominant, the Australian politicians and public servants responsible for engaging China will be put on the defensive, fearful of being labelled too China-friendly. They will constantly feel compelled to justify normal interactions in support of a constructive relationship. Stoking anti-China sentiment also risks alienating Chinese-Australian communities, a vital part of Australia's multi-cultural society.

As Australians look ahead to their future with China, they should always keep in mind the sanctity of long-held and fundamental principles, as these will surely be tested. This is a task for business, the media, educators, and indeed for all citizens. In preparation for that future, Australians should:

- **Demand their political leaders candidly acknowledge the potential erosion of Australian principles.** As Chinese government actors assert their influence in Australian society, elected officials starting with the prime minister should emphasise the non-negotiability of Australian democratic values and speak out against inappropriate and objectionable behaviour that undermines them.

- **Acquire far deeper knowledge of China's strategic objectives as it engages with Australian society.** This means investing in overall comprehension of Chinese politics, culture and society, especially for Australian citizens who are not of Chinese descent. Such knowledge will help Australians recognise unwelcome intrusions into our society, but temper unnecessary and detrimental suspicions.

- **Resist finger-pointing and seeing the hand of the PRC everywhere.** Overwrought mistrust only encourages xenophobic commentary and exacerbates tensions within already fragmented Australian-Chinese communities.

- **Support reforms to ban foreign donations to political activities.** This should be a priority for all political parties, as should transparent, regular and timely reporting of contributions.

- **Insist on academic freedom and integrity.** Australian educational institutions must remain platforms for respectful and vigorous debate, in which students and teachers feel comfortable defending their stances and are open to competing views. Any Chinese government attempt to censor classroom discussion and lower academic standards must be resisted. Financial pressures within the education sector should not be a reason to lower the bar for any student's entry or graduation.

- **Advocate for greater financial transparency within Australian institutions of learning, in particular regarding foreign**

philanthropy. Persons and institutions from the PRC have already made generous gifts to Australian schools, including A$100 million in 2016 from China's Ministry of Science and Technology for research at the University of New South Wales.[6] Far larger sums can be expected in the future. The education sector and society at large have an enormous stake in ensuring that donations, including those from China, do not impede freedom of inquiry and discussion.

- **Scrutinise partnerships with Chinese state-run media conglomerates which may restrict press freedom.** Readers, viewers and listeners need to be made aware of the source of the content they are provided by Australian media, as both big and small media outlets in Australia increasingly convey content directly taken from Chinese state-owned media sources. Far greater scrutiny and transparency are needed to avoid any inclination to self-censor. This is particularly true for Australian government-supported media such as the ABC and SBS.

- **Call out examples of Chinese government meddling that seeks to silence independent voices.** Australians should value independent Chinese-language media outlets and their contribution to a diverse array of opinion in Australia.

- **Shun business practices at odds with Australian principles and laws.** Corruption and bribery are widespread in China. Many PRC individuals may instinctively look to conduct business similarly in Australia. These cannot be accepted as a 'part of doing business'. The influx of Chinese businesspeople and investors will expand as economic ties with China deepen, putting intense pressure on Australian regulators and policing agencies. This will demand greater resources for oversight and law enforcement.

- **Reject claims by the Chinese government that Australian citizens born in the PRC can be dealt with and tried as PRC citizens when accused of committing crimes in China.** The Australian government must demand that all Australians, regardless of ancestry or place of birth, be treated as Australian citizens when they run afoul of the law in the PRC. They must be guaranteed access to Australian consular services.

Prosperity

Australia's future prosperity will depend heavily on an economic relationship with China that is markedly different from today's. But Australia is not ready for this.

The growth model which defined China's remarkable run of economic success over the past two decades is undergoing big changes. As recently as 2014 almost one-fifth of Australia's export earnings came from iron ore shipments to China, and mining exports overall made up nearly 30 per cent of total export earnings.[7] Those lucrative days of dependence on simple transactional relations – dropping off the goods at China's doorstep – are behind us. In the future, resource exports will remain important, but a new model of economic engagement with China is needed. Australians need to respond to the demand in China for a wide range of services. Australian business must build a larger beyond-the-border presence in China. Australia also needs to entice much more investment from China.

The change is already underway, with Austrade reporting that export of services to China rose from A$7.1 billion in 2013 to A$10.7 billion in 2016. Services exports to China already exceed the value of our iron ore exports to Japan and South Korea combined. But there is an even greater upside ahead. Research conducted by the Brookings Institution estimates that by 2030 the Chinese middle class will have grown by a staggering 850 million people.[8] As China's demand for services and consumer goods increases, the trade relationship will become less transactional and more reliant on people-to-people contact and the Australian 'brand'.

With the China–Australia Free Trade Agreement in force, the two countries will have greater access to each other's economies than ever before. That is good news, but far more needs to be done to improve Australian competitiveness in services. China is now the largest source of tourists for Australia and that surge has only just begun. This presents an enormous opportunity, but the Australian tourism sector is unprepared and will struggle to make the most of it. Language ability, cultural awareness and greater understanding of Chinese expectations are needed. If perceptions within China grow that Australia cannot absorb the rising flow of tourists and provide a valuable experience, those travellers will look elsewhere. Some Chinese tourists already complain about a lower standard of accommodation and infrastructure than in many other holiday destinations in the region. Australia ranks far down the list of preferred destinations for Chinese visitors on package tours, behind countries such as Vietnam, Indonesia and even Russia.[9]

Australians should not presume that Chinese-Australians can fill all the roles that require China conversancy and Mandarin proficiency. Not all Chinese-Australians want to be translators, tour guides, diplomats or business executives, nor should they be expected to. A lack of enthusiasm among most Australians to learn Mandarin holds the country back. In 2015, only 4000 Australian students graduated from Year 12 with Chinese-language qualifications, roughly 0.1 per cent of the total number of primary and secondary school students, and a mere 400 of those were not of Chinese heritage. The number of non-Chinese background pupils studying Chinese at Year 12 declined by 20 per cent between 2007 and 2015.[10] In New South Wales more students studied Latin than Chinese.

Chinese also represent by far the largest proportion of foreign students in Australia. For this to continue, educators will need to do more to ensure Chinese students return home with a high-quality degree, a positive experience and an affinity for Australia. At present many if not most of these students have little contact with Australian society. Government surveys reveal that Chinese students' satisfaction with opportunities to interact with Australians is consistently almost 10 per cent lower than the rest of international students in Australia.[11] Troublingly, their ability to converse in English tends to deteriorate while in Australia because they interact so little with English-speakers. For most Chinese students returning to China, their last contact with their university is graduation day. This is a lost opportunity. These students represent a potentially vast reservoir of goodwill and alumni support.

Investment is another case in point. Great opportunities lie ahead for Chinese investment in Australia. But Australians seem ambivalent about the prospect. With a relatively small population, Australia has always depended heavily on foreign investment for its prosperity – this is a point of near-universal agreement among political and business leaders. The need for Chinese investment is clear, yet news stories about the latest Chinese investment bid can send shock waves around the country, even though the PRC only accounts for about 2.5 to 3 per cent of Australia's total stock of foreign investment.[12] However, the targets of Chinese investment – real estate, infrastructure and agriculture – are often deemed politically sensitive.

This is a critically important issue because the composition of Chinese investment in Australia is shifting dramatically. According to Austrade, as late as 2013 some 95 per cent of Chinese investment in Australia was in metals and energy; by 2015 that figure had dropped to 30 per cent, as investors began to diversify into real estate, agriculture, transport, tourism and health. As of 2015, there was also a general tightening in China of capital controls. No state has felt the impact of this shift more than Western Australia. In 2012, Western Australia received 56 per cent of Chinese direct investment in Australia, principally in mining and energy. By 2015 that number had collapsed to 1 per cent.[13]

Australian prosperity is at risk if this major provider of capital is alienated on poorly considered political grounds. Agriculture is a good example. The shortfall between Australia's available domestic capital and what is required in agriculture will likely reach A$850 billion by 2050. Despite this, Australia is the fourth most restrictive place to invest in agribusiness out of thirty-five OECD countries.[14]

Remarkably, roughly 86 per cent of Australian farmland is Australian-owned and Australia produces enough food to feed 60 million people. Chinese investors rank fifth behind those from the United Kingdom, the United States, the Netherlands and Singapore in terms of foreign ownership of Australian agricultural land and hold less than a 0.4 per cent share. But there is no mistaking the demand from China: for the fiscal year 2014–2015,

China for the first time was the largest source of foreign investment in agriculture.[15] Nevertheless, public opposition to foreign investment in this sector is firm, with 69 per cent of Australians 'strongly against' the foreign acquisition of farmland, according to a Lowy Institute poll.

Inevitably, security concerns will become more intertwined with economic relations. Chinese investors will seek opportunities to invest in Australian infrastructure, agricultural holdings, real estate and other potentially sensitive assets. The overblown furore over the lease of the Port of Darwin to a Chinese company in 2015 is a case in point. Overlooked in the hubbub is the fact that Chinese state-owned companies already have very large stakes in other Australian ports – such as the Port of Newcastle, arguably a far more consequential facility for Australia's prosperity and security. Yet none of these port deals in fact presents a significant security risk for Australia.

In comparison, the rejection of two Chinese bidders for a minority stake in the NSW electricity distributor Ausgrid was based on valid security grounds. But the decision, coming late in the process, left a bad taste in the mouths of the Chinese investors, who had spent a lot of time and money on the understanding that their bids would go forward. It is true that the vast majority – close to 100 per cent – of Chinese investment applications are approved by the Foreign Investment Review Board (FIRB). However, one or two high-profile Chinese investments, especially if mismanaged and resulting in overhyped public reaction, can create the perception that Chinese investment is unwelcome.

The inconsistencies in federal and state policies are only adding to the miasma surrounding Chinese investment in infrastructure, real estate, agriculture and northern development. If Australia really is 'open for business', the government needs to make sure all potential investors know and believe this.

Uncertainty over how the PRC will exercise its power and influence in the region will undoubtedly exacerbate security concerns. Australians are also rightly concerned about preventing the infiltration of improper Chinese business practices at home and abroad. Nonetheless, business and government leaders need to do much more to foster a welcoming and transparent environment for Chinese investment. Chinese capital is not only important for Australia's future prosperity – having 'skin in the game' here could also encourage the PRC to have a greater stake in good relations with Australia and Australia's long-term success.

To make the most of economic relations with China in the future, Australians will need to:

- **Demand a more informed business leadership, willing and able to engage with national security decision-makers in Canberra.** For the two decades of the China resources boom, business got on with doing business while politicians and public servants in Canberra dealt with national security. Given the increasingly complex interaction of economic and security issues, this neat division of labour cannot continue. Prosperity is a part of national security. But there is a disconnect between business and government over the significance of economic ties with China for a stable and secure Australia. Business – traditionally at arm's length from Australian strategic and security decision-making – urgently needs to make itself heard. This requires CEOs not only making the effort to understand complex security issues, but also investing the time to convince decision-makers in Canberra of the merit of their economic arguments. The annual Australia–China CEO Roundtable Meeting should be reshaped with an eye to delivering candid conversation and meaningful recommendations on issues at the nexus of economics and security.

- **Welcome greater Chinese investment in Australia.** Politicians, public servants and corporate leaders must clearly articulate the facts and benefits of foreign investment in Australia, and the opportunities of Chinese investment in particular. More courageous political leadership is needed to convince the Australian public of the imperative of foreign investment. This will be particularly sensitive in the case of agribusiness, but it is precisely here where Australia holds profound advantages and Chinese investors will likely show most interest.

- **Seek reciprocity with the PRC.** Formal barriers to many Australian services exports remain high in China, especially in the financial and legal areas. As the China–Australia Free Trade Agreement matures, Australian investors will need promises of access to the China market to be honoured. Australians have a very strong interest in the Chinese government further opening up the market in several sectors, including finance, insurance, logistics, education and health. However, the demand for reciprocity should be applied judiciously so that it avoids self-defeating restrictions on Chinese investment in Australia.

- **Reform and clarify approval processes of the Foreign Investment Review Board.** Foreign investors the world over seek transparency, consistency and predictability. The FIRB should re-establish robust pre-application consultation so that prospective investors can make early 'go or no-go' determinations on specific projects. Regarding Chinese investment in particular, the FIRB will need to develop greater China-specific expertise. For example, as Chinese state-owned enterprises are not all the same, there is a growing need to thoroughly assess the risks that a given Chinese state-owned enterprise investment may or may not pose to Australian interests.

- **Remove obstacles to leadership for individuals of Chinese descent.** Numerous studies point to a lack of diversity at the top of Australian enterprises. Today, as the economic relationship with China deepens, there are more people of Chinese ethnic descent living in Australia than ever before. Since 2011, Mandarin has been the second most widely spoken language in Australia. These individuals are an immense pool of talent and bicultural knowledge which cannot be overlooked. Nevertheless, discrimination persists: according to a survey by the Scanlon Foundation in 2015, 25 per cent of Chinese-born immigrants to this country had met with discrimination in Australian society. Private enterprise and public institutions should redouble their efforts to ensure that these people have a fair opportunity to advance to high leadership positions.

- **Invest in Chinese language and cultural literacy.** Australia needs a far greater number of China-conversant and Mandarin-proficient citizens. This investment must be maintained over many decades. Reliance on Chinese-born Mandarin speakers can create its own challenges, hence the need to increase the number of Mandarin-fluent Australians of all ethnic backgrounds. This will be especially important in two ways: first, to support services in Australia, such as tourism and education; and second, to achieve a larger Australian business presence in China through investment and joint ventures.

- **Recognise the tremendous value of education as an export, but manage the risks.** The education sector holds enormous promise for Australia, but risks abound. The sector, especially at the higher levels, frets about over-dependence on the China market, struggles to maintain high academic standards in the face of insufficient English-language proficiency among Chinese international students, and risks losing its reputation as a preferred education provider due to many university administrators' tendency to view international students as cash cows. One highly publicised case of 'soft marking' of a Chinese student's exam would tarnish the entire Australian education sector. To remain competitive, the higher education sector in Australia needs to invest more in the student experience by dramatically expanding opportunities to interact with Australian society and business. Post-graduation engagement and alumni relations with Chinese students need to be strengthened. In the future, Chinese students should have access to an array of Australian courses, certificates and degree programs *in China* through a range of online and other remote learning platforms.

- **Elevate education to one of the most significant elements of the two countries' relationship.** Though education is one of Australia's top export earners, it is rarely appreciated or treated as such. Education should figure more prominently in the strategic dialogue between the two countries and be given high visibility during senior leaders' visits.

- **Strengthen opportunities for science and technology collaboration.** In several fields of research – such as mathematics, engineering and chemistry – China is now Australia's leading partner in collaboration, according to former Australian chief scientist Ian Chubb. He also notes that China is the second most important partner in agriculture, veterinary science, and immunology. Efforts should be made to increase interaction between Australian and Chinese researchers in science and technology fields at both universities and within the commercial sector.

- **Gear up to attract the burgeoning number of Chinese travellers and provide them with an extraordinary holiday experience.** Even as China becomes the number one source of holiday visitors to this country, Australia's tourism industry lacks the capacity and cultural agility to take full advantage of this opportunity. At present less than 1 per cent of China's 120 million outbound tourists come to Australia.

Security

Unlike Japan in World War II, China is highly unlikely to threaten Australian territory with military force. Hostile Chinese gunboats off the shores or in the harbours of Australia are not a serious prospect. Rather, Chinese threats are more nuanced and in many ways more difficult to defend against.

Take Australian cyber security, which entails safeguarding sensitive technologies, programs and data from damage and unauthorised access. China could disable or disrupt vital infrastructure or capture the sensitive government data of Australia or its allies and friends.

In the event of a conflict, this confidential information could be used against Australia or its partners.

A more palpable security threat is the likelihood that China would turn to economic forms of hard power. On a regular basis Chinese officials in face-to-face meetings formally express their strong disagreement with certain Australian actions they see as contrary to China's interests. The most sensitive issues for the Chinese government include Australian government engagement with Taiwanese officials, direct involvement in the South China Sea, support of Japan's more active security role in the region, and criticism of anything related to China's domestic situation, including measures to restrict freedom of expression. Even the activities of Falun Gong in Australia have been condemned by Chinese officials.

Looming over these discussions is the possibility of China resorting to economic threats and punishments. Measures could include restricting Australian agriculture exports to China under a regulatory pretence or 'new guidelines', limiting the number of Chinese tour groups to Australia, refusing licences for Australian business activities in China, and, worse still, discouraging Chinese students from attending Australian schools and universities.

Moreover, China's regional activities could pose a security risk to Australia. While not directly aimed at Australia, some of China's coercive actions towards its smaller neighbours – for example, sinking Coast Guard vessels or occupying disputed shoals – raise the possibility of a conflict, which would have repercussions for Australia. At worst, Australia could be drawn into a regional conflict in support of its friends, in particular its treaty ally the United States. Such a conflict could also disrupt commercial shipping to China, Japan, Taiwan and South Korea, markets on which Australian prosperity so heavily depends. As a relatively small country, Australia's security relies on an agreed-upon set of international rules. When China uses coercive measures to impose its will on others without negotiating a new, mutually acceptable set of rules, the security of the entire region becomes more tenuous.

In responding to many of these threats, Australia has been able to rely on its ally the United States for support. With access to US intelligence, Australia is in a far stronger position than it would be alone to counter cyber attacks and monitor the Chinese navy in the South China Sea and the maritime approaches north of Australia. Acquisition of some of the most advanced American defence technologies and the ability to operate jointly with US forces give Australia a military edge it would not otherwise have. Yet if China chooses to punish Australia economically, the United States would be of little help.

The US alliance also adds to the complexity of Australia's relationship with China. On the one hand, Australia's importance to China in the security sphere derives in part from its status as a US treaty ally. Through interactions with their Australian counterparts, Chinese officials glean insights into the United States and its strategic intentions and take the pulse of other US security relationships in the region. China recognises Australia's value to the United States as a significant intelligence partner and as a base for US and Australian joint military activities and logistical support.

On the other hand, there are four principal downsides – some would describe them merely as constraints – for Australia's China ties arising from this close partnership with the United States. A genuinely strategic partnership between Australia and China will always be hindered by China's mistrust of a close US ally. Second,

Australia will always be cautious with China to avoid perceptions of disloyalty to the alliance. Third, Australia is the target for more intensive Chinese attention, including through espionage, cyber attacks and military contingency planning, because of its close relationship with the United States.

Fourth, and most importantly, the alliance too often narrows the options for an independent Australian foreign policy. Donald Trump's ascent to the White House will further complicate Australian foreign and security policy. Some see this as a real opportunity for Australia to rethink the nature of its alliance relationship. Others see it in more stark terms and say Australia now has no choice but to forge its own independent foreign policy.

China's rise and Trump's election have created new and unfamiliar pressures for Australian foreign policymakers. Australia's leaders must now be far more frank with the Australian people about the challenges they face: the continuous need to balance the imperatives imposed by the US alliance with advancing a more constructive relationship with China.

These new challenges require Australians to:

- **Reject the simplistic mindset that sees China only in economic terms and the United States only in security terms.** This means avoiding the trap of a black-and-white choice of exclusively partnering with the United States or with China. Australian leaders need to make clear that both countries are critically important to Australia's security *and* prosperity. China not only contributes to Australia's security through its significant international peacekeeping and anti-piracy operations. Its four-decade pursuit of wealth has also significantly contributed to the absence of inter-state conflict and enabled the focus across the Asia-Pacific on internal development. The United States is the largest investor in Australia, with a total stock of A$860 billion as of 2015 (more than ten times the PRC investment). At the same time, the United States is the top destination for Australian investment overseas.

- **Alter the perception that Australia automatically follows the United States on regional issues related to China.** By doing so, Australia can expect to be perceived by China as a more credible regional actor. Even the use of language matters. Repeating American terminology is not helpful. The government in Canberra should resist pressure from Washington to take measures contrary to Australian interests. For example, Australia should have joined the Asian Infrastructure Investment Bank earlier. Australia should also continue to carry out independent maritime and aerial patrols in the South China Sea but not join the United States in conducting these operations. Australia needs to be in a stronger position to engage with China and encourage its support for regional rules and norms, which would also be in the interests of the United States, Japan and other friends. In the words of Richard Woolcott forty years ago, Australia must maintain 'an independent foreign policy within the framework of the alliance'.[16] Fast-forward to 2016 and Paul Keating captured the essence of this recommendation: 'We always need to be ready to tell the Chinese, or the Americans, that a particular approach or action is not in Australia's interests and that we won't go along.'[17]

- **Rebuff the view that the United States does not support strong, multifaceted ties between Australia and China.** It is not in

American interests for Australia to choose between the United States and China. In the words of a Pentagon spokesperson, that is 'a false choice'.[18] Australian leaders should continue to make clear to the Trump administration the fundamental importance of maintaining this position.

- **Tread carefully when it comes to contentious issues between China and Japan.** Owing to historical animosities and rising nationalist tendencies in China and Japan, citizens and governments alike too often take steps that unnecessarily provoke each other. The result is increasingly tense and unstable relations between the two Asian powers, a situation very much contrary to Australian interests. While Australia's influence is limited, it can only hope to be effective by taking an even-handed approach, calling for restraint, yet being willing to call out and criticise actions by either side that undermine regional stability.

- **Seek a new platform with Indonesia through which to interpret and shape China's regional actions.** This would entail a significant rethinking of Australia's ties with Indonesia to include a far stronger focus on China's regional ambitions and agreement on a coordinated set of policies and actions in response. The two governments should establish a China-focused working group and support non-governmental organisations to increase joint China-focused research and dialogue. There is much to be learned from countries with centuries of experience dealing with their big neighbour China, such as Vietnam and South Korea. But it is in Australia's interests to deepen its relations with Indonesia in particular, as Australia's closest ASEAN neighbour and a potential regional power.

- **Draw China into stronger regional security cooperation by establishing a new disaster relief body.** A new Humanitarian Assistance and Disaster Relief centre for the Asia-Pacific region should be established in the Northern Territory. Providing China, Indonesia, the United States, Australia and others in the region with the opportunity to train together would take Australia–China defence ties to a new level. It would also increase China's stake in regional security cooperation.

- **Insist on China keeping its commitment to a Comprehensive Strategic Partnership with Australia.** This means maintaining the annual leaders' meeting and regular dialogues between the prime minister, the foreign minister, the treasurer and their counterparts in China. Moreover, cyber security should be introduced as a key focus of these fora.

- **Energise the annual Australia–China High-Level Dialogue.** This gathering brings government officials together with business, academic, media and social leaders from both countries and should be a valued opportunity to discuss new and unconventional ideas. Over-ritualisation and formality should be avoided. By reducing the number of participants and focusing the agenda on a few sensitive issues, the meeting should recommend measures to tackle some of the more difficult problems in the relationship.

- **Invest far greater resources in understanding China's strategic thinking and decision-making.** Given the importance of China to Australia's prosperity and security, it is surprising how few Australians are formally trained in assessing China's strategic ambitions, whether in defence, security or foreign affairs.

Opportunities should be expanded considerably for Australian military and civilian experts to spend prolonged periods at Chinese institutions, including military academies and strategic studies centres. Chinese-language proficiency among a greater number of public servants, military officers and experts is an absolute necessity.

- **Exert more effort to understand the depth and complexity of US–China ties.** Too much attention is paid to the security dimensions of the relationship without a full understanding of the interdependent nature of the US–China relationship, which tempers the risk for conflict. US-based China watchers are world-class, but Australians should also closely follow analyses by authoritative Chinese US-watchers.

Think big!

Australia needs to rethink its relationship with China across the board. This means thinking big – thinking strategically and for the long term. It is an undertaking that requires the full engagement of Australian society: politicians, public servants, military officers, business, education, youth and community associations. What is needed now is a comprehensive, consistent strategy built on the three pillars of engagement: principles, prosperity and security.

Making China the focus of a regular whole-of-cabinet meeting is a big idea. A meeting of this kind, which focuses on a comprehensive approach to China, has not been convened for over a decade. Now that the National Security Committee has approved the government's new China strategy, it is imperative to have a discussion that brings together all ministers of the governing Coalition. In the same way, key federal department secretaries should convene on a regular basis to exclusively discuss China.

Second, Australian governments and businesses should jointly support the establishment of a long-term, extensive exchange program for the next generation of Australian and Chinese rising stars. Australian participants should be senior state and federal officials, promising backbenchers and future CEOs, among others. China's participants should include vice-governors and provincial deputy party secretaries, deputy mayors of major Chinese cities and future business leaders.

Held twice a year, once in Australia and once in China, this intensive program would provide firsthand experience of both countries' political and economic landscapes and create professional networks and personal friendships. For Australians, it will mean interacting with men and women who in the next ten years will rise to paramount positions of power in China. It is in Australia's interests that at least one of China's top leaders in 2027 has an intimate knowledge of Australia.

Third, Australia needs a national peak body with a mandate to advance the Australia–China relationship as it enters an unpredictable and challenging era. This organisation should serve as an honest broker and a reliable safety net, even when inevitable tensions put enormous pressure on the relationship. With people-to-people ties as its focus, its activities should include a national lecture series, workshops, retreats and educational programs in Australia and China. It should draw together the experience and knowledge of innumerable Australians and Chinese who have over the years created the remarkable dynamic between the two countries.

Such an organisation would be useful to Australia because it would offer a trusted but unofficial forum for visiting Chinese leaders to engage with Australian experts and the broader public. It could even assume responsibility for the Australia–China High-Level Dialogue and other fora to ensure frank discussions in an informal setting. Its funding should derive from both government and private sources, including corporations and foundations. Strong statutes and a mandate for autonomy should be put in place to keep this body independent of either government.

Fourth, Asian literacy needs to be institutionalised. Learning about Asian cultures and societies should be made compulsory from Year 1 onward. This initiative is not merely about learning Asian languages – though this is a critical component. Rather, this big idea has as its aim that every Australian child and young adult, regardless of their talents and particular path, should gain a deeper knowledge of the cultures and societies of Asia – Australia's home region. An Asian literacy course should also be compulsory for all university undergraduate students.

Within the Australian curriculum, Asian literacy ought to be embedded as a stand-alone subject within the Humanities and Social Sciences learning area. This will prepare Australians for a future in which Asia, and China in particular, will be of overwhelming significance. Another outcome of this ongoing Asia education would be to counter potential xenophobia and racism grounded in ignorance.

This big idea does not focus specifically on China. But a richer understanding of Asian cultures and societies will inescapably generate a deeper appreciation among Australians of China's historically prominent influence as well as its role and ambitions in the region today.

But thinking big is not enough. Big ideas demand leadership, determination and a long-term vision. A strong endorsement from the prime minister for a new approach to China is imperative, but that too is not enough. Ultimately it is up to leaders and citizens across society to transform Australia's engagement with China. That begins with understanding that China matters more and more for the things that Australians value most: principles, prosperity and security. Getting China right is more important than ever before.

Endnotes

INTRODUCTION

1   Rosie Blau, 'The new class war', *The Economist*, 9 July 2016. McKinsey Global Institute provides an empirical definition of China's middle class as households with an annual income of us$11,500–43,000. Other estimates of the size of China's middle class range from 109 to 500 million households.

2   National Farmers' Federation, 'China-Australia FTA great for Australian jobs, industry groups say', 31 August 2015.

3   Bernard Salt, 'Move over New Zealand, here comes the Chinese middle class', *The Australian*, 15 September 2016.

4   Sister Cities Australia, 'Directory of Australian sister city affiliations, 2016', June 2016, pp. 25–41.

5   Office of the Secretary of Defense, 'Annual Report to Congress: Military and Security Developments Involving the People's Republic of China 2016', 26 April 2016, p. 25.

6   Peter Ferdinand, 'Westward ho – the China dream and "One Belt, One Road" – Chinese foreign policy under Xi Jinping', *International Affairs* vol. 92, no. 4, 2016, pp. 947–8.

1. THE CHINA DREAM

1   The World Bank, 'GDP per capita (current us$), China', *World Bank DataBank, 2016.*

2   Evan Osnos, *Age of Ambition: Chasing Fortune, Truth, and Faith in the New China*, New York: Farrar, Straus and Giroux, 2014, p. 1.

3   The World Bank, 'GNI per capita, Atlas method, World', *World Bank DataBank*, 2016.

4   The World Bank, 'GNI per capita, Atlas method, China', *World Bank DataBank*, 2016.

5   The World Bank, 'Poverty and Equity Country Dashboard: China', *World Bank Group*, 2016.

6   Dominic Barton, Yougang Chen & Amy Jin, 'Mapping China's middle class', *McKinsey Quarterly*, June 2013, p. 3.

7   Ibid.

8   Cheng Li, *Chinese Politics in the Xi Jinping era: Reassessing Collective Leadership*, Washington, D.C.: Brookings Institution Press, 2016, p. 11.

9   Xi Jinping, 'Full text of Xi's address to the media, 18th National Congress of the Communist Party of China', *China Daily*, 16 November 2012.

10 William Callahan, 'History, identity, and security: Producing and consuming nationalism in China', *Critical Asian Studies*, vol. 38, no. 2, 2006, pp. 179–180.

11 Zheng Wang, 'Not rising, but rejuvenating: The Chinese Dream', *The Diplomat*, 5 February 2013.

12 Orville Schell & John Delury, *Wealth and Power: China's Long March to the Twenty-first Century*, New York: Random House, 2013.

13 Suisheng Zhao, 'Foreign policy implications of Chinese nationalism re-visited: The strident turn', *Journal of Contemporary China*, vol. 22, no. 82, 2013, p. 537.

14 Linda Jakobson, *China's unpredictable maritime security actors*, Lowy Institute for International Policy, December 2014, p. 29.

15 National Tourism Administration, *The Yearbook of China Tourism Statistics 1996*, Beijing: China Tourism Press, 1997, p. 20.

16 Richard Wike & Bridget Parker, 'Corruption, pollution, inequality are top concerns in China', *Pew Research Center*, 24 September 2015, pp. 2–4.

17 Yu quoted in Suthichai Yoon, 'The China Dream. What does it really mean?', *The Nation*, 1 August 2013.

2. SOCIAL CHANGE

1   National Bureau of Statistics of China, 'Table 4-2 Number of employed persons at year-end in urban and rural areas', *China Statistical Yearbook*

2015. Statistics in Chapter 2 about the Chinese population are taken from this official yearbook unless otherwise specified.

2   Tom Miller, *China's Urban Billion: The Story Behind the Biggest Migration in Human History*, New York: Zed Books, 2012, p. 3.

3   Jun Yang, 'An examination of China's New Urbanisation Strategy', *UGEC Viewpoints*, 19 January 2016. Cited in Robert A. Rohde & Richard A. Muller, 'Air pollution in China: Mapping of concentrations and sources', *PLOS ONE*, vol. 10, no. 8, 20 August 2015.

4   Jonathan Kaiman, 'China says more than half of its groundwater is polluted', *The Guardian*, 23 April 2014.

5   Xia Lingyin, 'Horizon Research survey report: Four mentality changes in Chinese society in the last 20 years', *Nanfang Zhoumo* [*Southern Weekly*], 31 August 2014.

6   Dexter Roberts & Jasmine Zhao, 'This is how China preps for the big test', *Bloomberg Businessweek*, 3 June 2016.

7   Credit Suisse Research Institute, 'Table 1 Change in the number of millionaires by country, 2014–15', *Credit Suisse Global Wealth Report 2015*, October 2015, p. 26.

8   The World Bank, 'Growing challenges', *East Asia and Pacific Economic Update*, April 2016, p. 50.

9   The World Bank, 'GINI Index (World Bank Estimate)', *World Bank DataBank*, 2016.

10   The Gini coefficient measures inequality on a scale of 0 (perfectly equal) to 1 (perfectly unequal); any country with a Gini coefficient over 0.5 is considered highly unequal. China's Gini coefficient peaked to 0.49 in 2008, but has gradually declined in the following seven years.

11   United Nations Development Programme, 'Inequality-adjusted Human Development Index', *Human Development Report*, 2015, p. 216.

12   National Bureau of Statistics of China, 'Update 2Q 2016 Quarterly by province: People's living conditions: Income and consumption expenditures', *National Data*, 2016.

13   Heather Timmons, 'China's regional economic growth', *The Atlas Charts*, 2 November 2015.

14   Gunter Schucher, 'The fear of failure, youth employment problems in China', *International Labour Review*, 21 October 2015.

15   David Barboza, 'Chinese man who bragged of privilege gets six years', *New York Times*, 30 January 2011.

16 'Xi Jinping millionaire relations reveal fortunes of elite', *Bloomberg News*, 29 June 2012.

17 Jane Perlez, 'Q. and A.: Henry Paulson on "dealing with China"', *New York Times*, 24 April 2015.

18 Mu Xuequan, 'Zhou Yongkang arrested, expelled from CPC', *Xinhua News Agency*, 6 December 2014.

19 James T. Areddy & Yang Jie, 'China's anticorruption campaign will continue, party watchdog pledges', *Wall Street Journal*, 25 January 2016.

20 Ibid.

21 '37 ministerial level Chinese officials investigated for graft in 2015', *Xinhua News Agency*, 3 January 2016.

22 The Asia Society, 'Infographic: Visualising China's anti-corruption campaign', *ChinaFile Database*, 21 January 2016. Updated 22 September 2016.

23 Ibid.

24 Yu Peiyang & Anne Henochowicz, 'Translation: Why Xi's anti-graft campaign bores me', *China Digital Times*, 26 September 2016.

25 Hudson Lockett, 'China anti-corruption campaign backfires', *Financial Times*, 10 October 2016; Ni Xing & Li Zhu, 'Perceptions of government integrity: Patterns of difference and its and explanation – based on a 2015 annual national survey on government integrity', *Journal of Public Administration*, vol. 9, no. 3, 2016.

26 Cheng Li & Ryan McElveen, 'Debunking misconceptions about Xi Jinping's anti-corruption campaign', *China-US Focus*, 17 July 2014.

27 Chun Han Wong, '"Today's kings without crowns?" – The growing powers of Xi's party disciplinarians', *Wall Street Journal*, 2 March 2016.

28 Ibid.

29 Anne-Marie Brady, 'Xi Jinping's challenge is to be strong enough to loosen control', *Financial Times*, 25 March 2015.

30 'China's Xi underscores CPC's leadership in news reporting', *Xinhua News Agency*, 19 February 2016.

31 Daniel Hurst, Katharine Murphy & Tania Branigan, 'Tony Abbott lauds Xi Jinping's "commitment to fully democratic China"', *The Guardian*, 18 November 2014.

32 Yu Keping, *Democracy and the Rule of Law in China*, Leiden: Brill, 2010, p. 8.

33 Suisheng Zhao, 'Xi Jinping's Maoist revival', *Journal of Democracy*, vol. 27, no. 3, July 2016, p. 84.

34 Brady, 'Xi Jinping's challenge'.

35 Cheng Li, *Chinese Politics in the Xi Jinping Era: Reassessing Collective Leadership*, Washington, D.C.: Brookings Institution Press, 2016, p. 397.

3. CHINA'S ECONOMIC TRANSITION

1 Robert Wade, *Governing the Market: Economic Theory and the Role of Government in East Asian Industrialization*, Princeton: Princeton University Press, 1990. See also Joe Studwell, *How Asia Works: Success and Failure in the World's Most Dynamic Region*, London: Profile Books, 2014.

2 Arthur R. Kroeber, *China's Economy: What Everyone Needs to Know*, Oxford: Oxford University Press, 2016, pp. 210–232.

3 Ibid., p. 167.

4 Nicholas R. Lardy, *Markets Over Mao, The Rise of Private Business in China*, Washington, D.C.: Peterson Institute for International Economics, 2014.

5 Organisation for Economic Co-operation and Development, 'OECD Economic Surveys: China', March 2015, p. 26. See also Richard Herd, 'The fall of productivity and the rise of debt', *China Economic Quarterly*, vol. 20, no. 1, March 2016, pp. 17–26.

6 Barry Naughton, 'Reform agenda in turmoil: Can policy-makers regain the initiative?', *Chinese Leadership Monitor*, no. 48, 9 September 2015; 'Supply-side structural reforms: Policy-makers look for a way out', *Chinese Leadership Monitor*, no. 49, 1 March 2016; 'Two trains running: Supply-side reform, SOE reform and the authoritative personage', *Chinese Leadership Monitor*, no. 50, 19 July 2016; 'Supply-side structural reform at mid-year: Compliance, initiative, and unintended consequences', *Chinese Leadership Monitor*, no. 51, 30 August 2016.

7 World Bank and Development Research Center of the State Council, 'China 2030: Building a modern, harmonious and creative society', Washington, D.C.: World Bank, 2013.

8 International Monetary Fund, 'Staff Report for the 2016 Article IV Consultation', 7 July 2016. See also Tom Mitchell, 'World Bank warns China to reform 'distorted' financial system', Financial Times, 1 July 2015; and Tom Mitchell, 'World Bank backtracks on China criticism', *Financial Times*, 17 July 2015.

9   Richard Koo, *The Holy Grail of Macroeconomics: Lessons from Japan's Great Recession*, Singapore: John Wiley & Sons, 2009.

10 If the European Union is treated as a single trading bloc, China would be the largest trading partner to around thirty-five countries. See data compiled from the *CIA World Factbook* at https://en.wikipedia.org/wiki/List_of_the_largest_trading_partners_of_China. See also David Yanofsky, 'Globalisation Really Means Countries Just Trade With Their Neighbours', *Quartz*, 26 February 2014.

11 Australian Government Department of Foreign Affairs and Trade, 'Australia's Direction of Goods & Services Trade – Calendar Year (From 1987 to Present)', Trade Time Series Data.

12 Australian Bureau of Statistics, 'International Investment Position, Australia: Supplementary Statistics, 2015 – Table 1 and Table 2.', Catalogue 5352.0, 13 May 2016.

4. THE SOFT SIDE OF CHINESE POWER

1   Wanning Sun, 'Chinese-Language Media in Australia: Developments, Challenges and Opportunities', Australia-China Relations Institute, 8 September 2016, pp. 67–69.

2   Australian Government Department of Education and Training, 'The 10th Confucius Institute Conference held in Shanghai', 21 December 2015.

3   Russell Flannery, 'Inside The 2016 Forbes List of China's 400 Richest People: Wang Jianlin Repeats at No. 1', *Forbes Asia*, 26 October 2016.

4   Fu Ying, 'What are the U.S. and China fighting over?', *Bloomberg News*, 1 September 2016.

5   Quoted in Philip Wen, 'China's propaganda arms push soft power in Australian media deals', *Sydney Morning Herald*, 31 May 2016.

6   Sun, 'Chinese-Language Media in Australia', p. 5.

7   Wen, 'China's propaganda arms'.

8   John Fitzgerald, 'Why values matter in Australia's relations with China', *The Asan Forum*, 13 June 2014.

9   'ABC and the Great Firewall of China', *Media Watch*, ABC, Episode 15 transcript, 9 May 2016.

10 Philip Wen, 'China's patriots among us: Beijing pulls new lever of influence in Australia', *Sydney Morning Herald*, 14 April 2016.

11 Georgia Behrens, 'Spies in Sydney Uni: Really?' *Honi Soit*, 28 April 2014.

12 Yu Zhengsheng, head of the Chinese People's Political Consultative Conference, quoted in 'Top political advisor stresses uniting overseas Chinese', *Global Times*, 11 October 2013.

13 James Jiann Hua To, *Qiaowu: Extra-Territorial Policies for the Overseas Chinese*, Leiden: Brill, 2014.

14 Eva O'Dea, 'The PRC's engagement with Australian society: how should Australia respond?', discussion paper presented at Second National Meeting of China Matters, 20 November 2015.

15 Ibid.

16 John Garnaut, 'Chinese Spies at Sydney University', *Sydney Morning Herald*, 21 April 2014; Fitzgerald, 'Why values matter', 2014; Rowan Callick, 'Tibetans in Australia "monitored by China"', *The Australian*, 29 January 2014.

17 Georgia Behrens, 'Spies in Sydney Uni: Really?' *Honi Soit*, 28 April 2014.

18 Linton Besser, Clay Hichens & Mario Christodoulou, 'Australian-Chinese businessman Michael Li claims China intimidation after refusing to act as spy', *ABC News Four Corners*, 12 October 2015.

19 Philip Wen, Eryk Bagshaw & Kate Aubusson, 'University of Sydney tutor Wu Wei resigns after calling students "pigs"', *Sydney Morning Herald*, 18 April 2016.

20 Philip Wen, 'Jailed executives are Chinese, Carr told', *Sydney Morning Herald*, 15 May 2012.

21 Enda Curran, 'Stokes slams Canberra over US troops decision', *Australian Business Review*, 14 September 2012.

22 Drawn from donor annual returns for 2012–2013, 2013–2014 and 2014–2015 at the Australian Electoral Commission website.

23 Chris Uhlmann, Andrew Greene & Stephanie Anderson, 'Chinese donors to Australian political parties: Who gave how much?', *ABC News*, 21 August 2016.

24 Primrose Riordan, 'Sam Dastyari-linked political donor resigns from Bob Carr institute after major review', *Australian Financial Review*, 21 September 2016.

25 Stephen FitzGerald, 'China's deepening engagement in Australian society: Is it a concern?', discussion paper presented at Fourth National Meeting of China Matters, 22 September 2016.

26 Ibid.

27 Linda Jakobson, 'Beware the China alarmists out there', *The Australian*, 23 September 2016.

28 Ibid.

5. CHINESE HARD POWER

1 See the joint statement and foreign minister remarks at the Norwegian government website, 'Full normalisation of relations with China', Ministry of Foreign Affairs press release, 19 December 2016.

2 Michael Kohn, 'Mongolia vows no more Dalai Lama visits after China turns screws', *Bloomberg*, 22 December 2016.

3 Andreas Fuchs & Nils-Hendrik Klann, 'Paying a visit: The Dalai Lama Effect on international trade', paper presented at Silvaplana 2010, 19th Workshop on Political Economy, July 2010.

4 Joseph Nye, 'Propaganda isn't the way: Soft power', *International Herald Tribune*, 10 January 2003.

5 The World Bank, 'Country Metadata: China', *World Bank DataBank, 2016*.

6 International Monetary Fund, 'International Monetary Fund World Economic Outlook Database', April 2016.

7 Jacopo Dettoni, 'Chinese R&D goes global', *Financial Times*, 31 August 2016.

8 Ernst & Young, 'Going out: The global dream of a manufacturing power: 2016 China outbound investment outlook', *Ernst & Young Report*, March 2016, p. 6.

9 These data are drawn from Stockholm International Peace Research Institute Military Expenditure Database and expressed in constant 2014 US dollars.

10 Office of the Secretary of Defense, 'Annual report to Congress: Military and security developments involving the People's Republic of China 2016', 26 April 2016, p. 30.

11 Linda Jakobson & Dean Knox, 'New foreign policy actors in China, SIPRI Policy Paper 26', Stockholm International Peace Research Institute, September 2010.

12 'Chinese tourists expected to drop 33 per cent', *The China Post*, 1 July 2016.

13 Amy King & Shiro Armstrong, 'Did China really ban rare earth metals exports to Japan?', *East Asia Forum*, 18 August 2013.

14 Wang Wen & Chen Xiaochen, 'Who supports China in the South China Sea and why', *The Diplomat*, 27 July 2016.

15 '"Paper Cat" Australia will learn its lesson', *Global Times*, 30 July 2016.

16 Philip Wen, 'China warns against threats to ties and investment from Australian "protectionism"', *Sydney Morning Herald*, 17 August 2016.

17 'Japan jet scrambles against Chinese aircraft hit six-month record', *Reuters*, 14 October 2016.

18 See the Chinese government white paper, State Council Information Office, *China adheres to the position of settling through negotiation the relevant disputes between China and the Philippines in the South China Sea*, 13 July 2016, pp. 1–3.

19 Linton Besser, Jake Sturmer & Ben Sveen, 'Government computer networks breached in cyber attacks as experts warn of espionage threat', *ABC News Four Corners*, 29 August 2016.

20 Central Intelligence Agency, 'East & Southeast Asia: China', *The World Factbook*, last updated 10 November 2016; The World Bank, 'Arable land (% of land area)', *World Bank DataBank*, 2016.

21 Ben Blanchard & John Ruwitch, 'China hikes defense budget, to spend more on internal security', *Reuters*, 5 March 2013.

22 'Who is most dependent on China?', *Bloomberg News*, 5 August 2016.

23 An important and detailed study of these issues is Michael S. Chase et al., 'China's incomplete military transformation: Assessing the weaknesses of the People's Liberation Army (PLA)', *RAND Corporation*, 2015. See also Dennis J. Blasko, 'Ten reasons why China will have trouble fighting a modern war', *War on the Rocks*, 18 February 2015.

24 'Will Trump start a trade war against China?', *Global Times*, 13 November 2016.

25 Bates Gill, Evelyn Goh & Chin-Hao Huang, 'The dynamics of US–China–Southeast Asia relations', *United States Studies Centre at the University of Sydney*, June 2016.

26 East Asian Bureau of Economic Research & China Center for International Economic Exchanges, 'Partnership for change: Australia-China joint economic report', Canberra: Australian National University Press, August 2016.

6. GETTING IT RIGHT FOR AUSTRALIA

1 Stephen Hutcheon, 'China lashes PM for meeting the Dalai Lama "Devil"', *Sydney Morning Herald*, 26 September 1996, p. 1.

2 Australian Bureau of Statistics, 'International Merchandise Trade, Australia, June 2001', Catalogue 5422.0, 17 August 2001.

3 Australian Government Department of Foreign Affairs and Trade, 'Trade at a glance 2011', 2011.

4 Barack Obama, 'Text of Obama's speech to Parliament', *Sydney Morning Herald*, 17 November 2011.

5   Stephen FitzGerald, 'China's deepening engagement in Australian society: is it a concern?', discussion paper presented at Fourth National Meeting of China Matters, 22 September 2016, p. 1.

6   The A$100 million donation is to establish a Torch Innovation Precinct at UNSW, the first outside of China. There are over 150 such projects in China. Research at the UNSW precinct will focus on advanced materials, biotechnology, energy and environmental engineering. Harry Tucker, 'The Chinese government is building an innovation campus at the University of New South Wales', *Business Insider*, 15 April 2016.

7   Australian Trade Commission, 'Trade and investment note: How dependent are Australian exports on China?', February 2015, p. 4.

8   Homi Kharas & Geoffrey Gertz, 'The new global middle class: A cross-over from west to east', *Wolfensohn Center for Development, Brookings Institution*, 2010.

9   Michael Heath, 'Holiday in Australia?: Chinese tourists would rather go to Russia', *Sydney Morning Herald*, 28 October 2016.

10 Jane Orton, 'Building Chinese language capacity in Australia', Australia-China Relations Institute, 20 April 2016, p. 42.

11 Australian Government Department of Education and Training, 'International Student Survey 2014', (unpublished data).

12 Australian Bureau of Statistics, 'International Investment Position, Australia: Supplementary Statistics, 2015', Catalogue 5352.0, 11 May 2016.

13 KPMG & The University of Sydney, 'Demystifying Chinese investment in Australia', *KPMG report*, April 2016, p. 16.

14 Organisation for Economic Co-operation and Development, 'OECD FDI Regulatory Restrictiveness Index', OECD Statistics.

15 Hannah Bretherton, 'Does Australia *really* welcome investment from China? A closer look at agribusiness in Western Australia and northern Australia', discussion paper presented at Fourth National Meeting of China Matters, 22 September 2016, p. 1.

16 Richard Woolcott, *The Hot Seat: Reflections on Diplomacy from Stalin's Death to the Bali Bombings*, Sydney: HarperCollins, 2003, p. 199.

17 Troy Bramston, 'Paul Keating lets fly at Labor over South China Sea', *The Australian*, 11 October 2016.

18 Tom Westbrook, 'Australia must choose between United States and China: U.S. Army official', *Reuters*, 1 September 2016.

Index

Abbott government 163
Abbott, Tony 56–7
Abe, Shinzo 137
academic freedom and integrity
    50–1, 54, 114, 116, 169
Age, The 102
ageing population 66, 83, 149
agribusiness, FDI in Australia 174–5
agricultural commodities 85, 87, 90
air defence identification zones
    (ADIZs) 143
air force 132–3
air pollution 37
Alibaba 94, 95
American Dream 31
anti-corruption campaigns 5–6, 30,
    44–9
anti-piracy operations 134, 154, 157,
    183
Asia-Pacific Economic Cooperation
    (APEC) 159
Asia-Pacific region
    China's relations within region
        123–4
    disaster relief body for 186
    US military presence and defence

relationships 137, 152
US 'pivot' strategy 27, 136, 161–2
US role under Trump 165
Asian Infrastructure Investment Bank
    (AIIB) 80, 131, 155, 184
Asian literacy, institutionalisation in
    Australia 189
Association of Southeast Asian
    Nations (ASEAN) 140
Ausgrid 141–2, 175
Austrade 146
Australia China Economics, Trade
    and Culture Association 112
Australia Plus website 106
Australia–China CEO Roundtable
    Meeting 177
Australia–China consular agreement
    117
Australia–China relations
    annual leadership dialogue 163,
        186
    building political trust 163
    challenges ahead 125, 164–6
    during Abbott government 163
    during Gillard government 118,
        161–3

Australia–China relations (*cont.*)
  during Howard government 160–1
  during Rudd government 161
  economic challenges and
    prosperity 176–80
  and exertion of soft power by PRC
    122–5, 167–71
  free trade agreement 163
  future engagement 159
  impact of US–Australia alliance
    141, 164, 165, 182–5
  impact of US–China relations 2,
    11–12, 118, 182
  interdependence 160
  peak body to advance relationship
    188–9
  principles to be upheld 166–71
  science and technology
    collaboration 180
  security challenges 183–7
  strategic partnership 163, 186
Australia–Indonesia relations 185
Australia-China Relations Institute
  (ACRI) 102, 120
Australian Broadcasting Corporation
  (ABC), *Australia Plus* website 106
Australian Council for the Promotion
  of Peaceful Reunification of China
  112, 119
Australian economy, impact of
  Chinese economy 6–7, 84–9
Australian Financial Review 102
Australian Labor Party (ALP), China-
  related donations to 119–20
Australian New Express Daily 105, 119
Australian Security Intelligence
  Organisation (ASIO) 146
Australian-Chinese business leaders
  108
Australian-Chinese community,
  responses to PRC propaganda 124

Behrens, Georgia 115
Beijing Olympic Games 27, 93, 113
Beijing Review 98
bilateral investment treaties (BITs)
  91–2
Bishop, Julie 164
boycotts 139
Brady, Anne-Marie 51
Bureau of Meteorology 146
business leadership in Australia,
  engagement with national security
  decision-makers 176–7

Callahan, William 20–1
Cambodia–China relations 140
capital accumulation 64, 67
capital investment 7, 63, 66
capital productivity 64, 67
Carr, Bob 120, 162
Ceaușescu, Nicolae 57
censorship 6, 106–7
Central Commission for Discipline
  Inspection (CCDI) 50–1, 54
Central Committee 70
Central Leading Group for
  Comprehensively Deepening
  Reforms 45
'century of humiliation' 4, 20–3, 28, 138
Chau Chak Wing 105, 119
Chau, Winky 105
ChemChina 131
Chen Shui-bian 135–6
Cheng Li 49
China Central Television (CCTV)
  98–9, 102–3, 107
China Coast Guard 24, 143, 157
China Daily 98, 102, 105, 123
China Development Bank (CDB) 131
China Dream
  compared to American Dream 31

defence of Chinese interests 23–6
dominance in Asia-Pacific 27
importance of understanding 3–4,
    16–18
mismatch with Australian dreams
    and aspirations 166–7
objectives 17–18
and personal dreams of citizens
    30–1
rejuvenation of Chinese nation
    18–23
resonance with Chinese people
    19–20, 28–9, 31
resources needed for fulfilment 29
respect from United States 26–8
Xi's ambitions and 16
China Global Investment Tracker
    (CGIT) database 87, 88–9
China Radio International (CRI) 98,
    102, 103
'China Watch' supplement 102, 105,
    123
China–Australia Free Trade
    Agreement 163, 172, 177
China–Mongolia relations 127–8
China–Norway relations 126–7
China.org.cn 98
Chinese air force 132–3
Chinese cultural heritage 20, 93
Chinese culture, influence of 8, 13
Chinese diaspora see overseas Chinese
Chinese embassies and consulates 97,
    113–14
Chinese immigrants 2, 178
Chinese navy 95, 133, 134
Chinese students abroad
    in Australia 173, 179
    corrupt practices 114, 116, 179
    PRC attempts to influence 112–14
    surveillance of 108
    in United States 27–8, 156

Chinese Students and Scholars
    Association (CSSA) 113
Chinese technology 94
Chinese-language media 99
Chinese-language proficiency in
    Australia 173, 178–9, 187, 189
Chubb, Ian 180
citizenship issues 117, 171
CNC World 102
collective leadership 44–5
commodities 84–8
Communist Party of China (CPC)
    China Dream concept 4
    corruption 40–1
    cynicism towards 28
    document no. 9 53
    future of 55–61
    impact of anti-corruption
        campaign 5
    as indispensable 23
    internal reforms 60
    leading small groups (LSGs) 45
    as saviours of China 20–1
    secrecy 3
Communist Party of the Soviet
    Union, collapse 57, 58
Confucius Classrooms 99
Confucius Institutes 99
consumer spending 67
corruption
    business dealings in Australia
        170–1
    campaigns against 5–6, 30, 44–9
    pervasiveness of 40
    public dissatisfaction with 36,
        40–1
crime 57–8
cyber attacks 145–7, 180–1
cyber espionage 145
cyber security 180–1, 186
cyber warfare 147

cyber weaponry 145, 147
cyberspace, military capabilities
133–4

'Dalai Lama Effect' 127–8, 160–1
Dalian Wanda Group 94
Dastyari, Sam 118–19, 120
Defence Science Technology Group
146
Delury, John 21
democracy, likelihood in China 56–7
democratic values, non-negotiability
of 168–9
Deng Xiaoping
approval for Chinese to study in
United States 27
on democracy in China 57
'hide and bide' strategy 135
instigation of reforms 16
pace of economic reform 30, 35, 36
principles of collective leadership
44
dependency ratio 65, 66
determinism 17
Diaoyu Islands 142–3, 152–3
disaster relief body for Asia-Pacific
region 186
Dominion Post (NZ) 105
Drysdale, Peter 159
Duterte, Rodrigo 144

East Asian developmental state model
65, 66
East China Sea
air defence identification zones
(ADIZs) 143, 153
displays of hard power 143
disputed islands 142–3, 152–3
economic clout 129–31, 155

economic coercion 10–11, 12, 138–42,
155–6, 181
economic growth
capital-intensive growth 7, 8, 63,
67
consumption-led growth 7, 8, 63,
67
East Asian developmental state
model 65, 66
since outset of reform era 129
slowdown in 39–40
sources 65
sustainability of 67–8
transition to new model 7, 63,
66–8
under 'failure to reform' scenario
76–8
under 'successful reform' scenario
73–6
economic leverage, wielding of 10–11,
12, 80–1, 138–42, 155–6, 181
economic policy in Australia,
adapting to changing Chinese
economy 89–92
economic reform
implicit social pact over 36
lack of progress 69–73
productivity-enhancing agenda
68–9
role of the market 8, 70–3
to avoid middle-income trap 64
economic stimulus program, in
2008–2009 66–7
economy
benefits and costs of rapid growth
62–3
global effects and influence 62–3,
64, 78–84, 129–31
gross debt to GDP ratio 68
impact on Australian economy
6–7, 84–9

implications for Australia
   economic policy 89–92
regional differences 39
in transition 62–4
see also names of sectors, e.g.
   services sector
education
   as Australian export 179
   place in Australia–China dialogue
     179
   see also Chinese students abroad
educational institutions, foreign
   philanthropy and financial
   transparency 169–70
educational opportunity 30
employment, loosening of controls
   over 32–4
energy market 84–5
English-language media 98
entrepreneurialism 33–4
environmental degradation 30, 37
equality, ideal of 37–8
equity market, government
   intervention 71–2
exports, China's reliance on 66

Fairfax Media 102, 123
Falun Gong 114, 116, 181
financial crisis
   possible international implications
     82–4
   potential for 76–8
financial deregulation 71
financial liberalisation 69
financial sector reform 71–3
fiscal reform 69
Fitzgerald, John 106, 115
FitzGerald, Stephen 167
Food Safety Law 43
food security 30, 43

foreign direct investment (FDI)
   by Australian firms in Chinese
     services 90–1
   by Chinese firms in Australia
     87–9, 91, 173–6, 177
   by US firms in Australia 184
   'greenfield' investments 131
   increase in outward FDI 131
foreign exchange market, government
   intervention 71, 72–3
Foreign Investment Review Board
   (FIRB) 175, 177–8
foreign policy, in Australia 183, 184
Four Comprehensives 45–6
Foxtel 107
freedom, increase in personal
   freedom 32–6
freedom of choice 16–17
freedom of movement 33, 57
freedom of the press 106–7, 170
freedom of speech 6, 47
Fu Ying 101

Garnaut, John 115
GDP, ratio of gross debt to 7
Gillard government
   alliance with United States 118,
     162
   relations with China 118, 161–2
Gillard, Julia
   on Australia–China relations 162–3
   on Australia–US relations 162
   visit to China 163
Gini coefficient 38, 194*n*10
Global China-Australia Media Group
   102
global financial crisis
   contributing factors 63
   impact on US–Chinese relations
     26–7

Global Times 98, 120, 141, 156
Great Firewall of China 51–2, 106
'greenfield' investments 131
gross debt to GDP ratio 68
Guo Boxiong 47

hard power
    against United States and its allies
        152–3, 156
    capacity to exercise it 129
    concept of 10, 128
    counteractive constraints 149–53
    economic coercion 10–11, 12,
        138–42, 155–6, 181
    future deployment 155–9
    military threats 10, 156
    and PLA's lack of operational
        experience 153–5
    shows of force 142–7, 181–2
    structural constraints on 147–9
    willingness to display and use it
        126–8, 134–8
Harmonious Society (slogan) 29
health care 30, 43
Hollywood movie industry 94–5, 105
household registration system 35
Howard government, relations with
    China 160–1
Howard, John, meeting with Dalai
    Lama 160
Hu Jintao 22, 29, 40, 44
Huang Xiangmo 119, 120
human rights 53, 106, 118, 127
human-rights lawyers and activists,
    detention of 52–3

imports
    from Australia 1–2, 86–8, 159
    restrictions on 138

income inequality 30, 37–9
Indonesia–Australia relationship 185
industrial sector 7
industrial upgrading 69
infrastructure development 7, 63
Inner Mongolia 148
internal security 149
international investment flows 63–4
international peacekeeping
    operations 95, 134, 157, 183
international students *see* Chinese
    students abroad
international tourism
    and exercise of soft power 138–9
    extent of 29, 63
    FDI in China-oriented tourism
        projects 91
    inbound flights to China 2
    to Australia 172–3, 180
internet surveillance and censorship
    51–2
internet usage 1, 6
Ishihara, Shintaro 142

Japan
    defence cooperation with United
        States 137, 152–3
    dispute with China over Senkaku/
        Diaoyu Islands 142–3, 152–3
    economic punishments inflicted
        by China 139
    'lost decade' 78, 82
    and regional stability 185
Jiang Zemin 22, 40, 57
judicial independence 59

Keating, Paul 184
Key, John 141
Kingold Group 105, 119

Koizumi, Junichiro 139
Kuomintang (KMT) 110

labour force, expansion 65
Law on Non-Governmental
    Organisations 52
Lee Teng-hui 135
legal reform 59
Li Gang 42
Li Keqiang 94
Li, Michael 115–16
Li Zhu 48
Liberal Party of Australia, China-
    related donations 119–20
Liu Qibao 101
Liu Xiaobo 126
Liu Yunshan 97
living standards 17, 37

Ma, Jack 94
'Made in China 2025' policy plan 69
Mandarin Chinese-speakers, in
    Australia 2, 172–3, 178
manufacturing comparative
    advantage 90
Mao Zedong era
    centralisation of power 44, 49
    equality in 37–8
maritime interests 4, 25
Maritime Silk Road 26
media
    avoidance of critical commentary
        105
    censorship 106–7
    Chinese media presence around
        the world 101–8
    Chinese-language media 99, 104–5
    English-language media 98–9
    online and mobile channels 1, 9, 104

partnerships with Chinese state-run
    conglomerates 102, 105, 106,
    107, 123, 170
media openness 6, 52
Media Watch 106
middle class 18, 192n1
Middle Kingdom, soft power 8
middle-income trap 64
military expenditure 11, 132, 149
military facilities 144, 156–7
military parade, Beijing, 2015 126
military strength and capabilities 2,
    11, 126, 132–4, 155–7
military threats 10, 11
mobile phones 1
Mongolia, Chinese retaliation for visit
    by Dalai Lama 127–8

national humiliation 20–1
National Museum of China, 'The
    Road to Renewal' exhibition 19
National Party, China-related
    donations 119
national pride 20, 22
national saving rate 63
National Security Committee (NSC)
    164, 187
National Security Law 52
nationalism 23, 28, 53, 137–8
New Development Bank (formerly
    BRICS Development Bank) 80, 131
New Express Daily (Guangzhou) 104
New Silk Road Fund (NSRF) 131
New Zealand–China relations 141
NewSat Ltd 146
Ni Xing 48
Nobel Peace Prize, to Liu Xiaobo
    126
non-governmental organisations
    (NGOs), surveillance of 52, 54

North Korea
    dependence on China 149–50
    economic pressure from China 150
    UN sanctions against 150
Norway, Chinese retaliation over
    Nobel Prize to dissident 126–7
Nye, Joseph 96, 128

Obama, Barack 27, 137, 153, 161–2
One Belt, One Road (OBOR) project
    25–6, 80, 84, 131, 151, 155
one-child policy 34–5
Osnos, Evan 17
overseas Chinese
    associations 111–12
    Chinese students abroad 112–14
    as 'fifth-column supporters' 109
    PRC government's efforts to
        influence 108–12
    PRC-born elites in foreign
        societies 111–12
    resident in Australia 108
    rights of PRC-born Australian
        citizens in China 117, 171
    size of diaspora 108
    as soft power targets 99
    surveillance and intimidation of
        114–17
    'the three knives' 110

Paracel Islands 144
parliamentary democracy 56–7
patriotism 20, 22
Peace Ark 95
'peaceful development' concept 135,
    136
'peaceful rise' concept 135, 136
Peng Liyuan 49, 94
People's Bank of China (PBOC) 63, 72

People's Daily Online 102
People's Liberation Army (PLA)
    air and sea power 132–3
    and anti-corruption campaign 5
    anti-piracy operations 134, 154,
        157, 183
    development of capabilities 155–7
    international peacekeeping
        operations 95, 134, 157, 183
    lack of operational experience
        153–4
    modernisation 132–4, 136
    Navy 95, 133, 134
    Peace Ark 95
    reorganisation 132
    Rocket Force 133
    space- and cyber-related
        capabilities 133–4
    voice in decision-making 138
per capita income 17–18
Permanent Court of Arbitration,
    ruling on China's maritime claims
    139–41, 143–4
personal freedom 32–6
philanthropy 99–100, 169–70
Philippines
    cyber attacks by China 146
    economic punishments inflicted
        by China 138
    Permanent Court of Arbitration
        case against China 139–40,
        143–4
    territorial claims in South China
        Sea 137, 138, 144
Politburo Standing Committee 45,
    61, 70, 97
political assertiveness 80–1, 86
political donations 119–20, 169
political instability, fear of 58
political and policy influence in
    Australia 118–21

political reform 56–8, 81
political slogans 28
popular nationalism 23
Port of Darwin 175
Port of Newcastle 175
poverty 18, 38
power, abuses of 41–3
principles, upholding in strategic
   engagement with China 166–71
private sector
   allocation of resources to 65, 66
   fixed asset investment 66
   role in Chinese economy 18
Propaganda Department
   aims 9–10
   censorship of internet 51
   crackdown on dissenters 52–3
   external portrayal and promotion
     of PRC 96–8
   name change in English 98
   resources 9

Qingdao Publishing Group 102
Qinghai region 148

racial discrimination, against Chinese
   immigrants 178
rare earth exports 139
'red princelings' 45
Regional Comprehensive Economic
   Partnership (RCEP) 159
regional security cooperation 186
regional stability, maintaining 185
reproductive rights 34–5
resource allocation
   role of market forces 68–9
   to private sector 65, 66–7
resource mobilisation 7
resources boom 86

rights protection 25
'The Road to Renewal' exhibition 19
Rudd government, relations with
   China 161
rule of law 6, 31
rural–urban migration 36, 57–8

Scarborough Shoal, dispute over 138,
   144, 146
Schell, Orville 21
science and technology collaboration
   180
security environment
   Chinese contribution to
     Australian security 183–4
   future challenges in Australia–
     China relations 180–7
   interaction of economic and
     security issues 175–7
   and protection of Chinese
     interests 136–7
   regional security cooperation 186
   US 'pivot' strategy in Asia-Pacific
     27, 136, 161–2
security and surveillance laws 52–3
Senkaku/Diaoyu Islands 142–3,
   152–3
service exports, from Australia to
   China 90, 172, 177
service market, access to 91–2
service trade deficit 90
services sector
   growth in 7
   investment by Australian firms in
     90–1
   share of GDP 67
Shambaugh, David 101
Shanghai Expo 93
Shanghai Free Trade Zone (FTZ) 91,
   92

Silk Road 26
sister city/sister state relationships 2
Sky News Australia 102
social equality, growing disparities 5
social injustice 30–1, 41–3
social media, surveillance and
    censorship 51
social media platforms 1, 9, 104
social media use 1
social mobility 37, 40
social status, disparities in 37
soft power
    Chinese media presence 101–8
    concept of 8, 95–6
    outreach by PRC government
        96–101, 167
    political and policy influence
        117–21
    responding to PRC government's
        strategies in Australia 121–5,
        167–71
    through overseas Chinese
        communities 108–17
    use by Propaganda Department
        9–10, 96–8, 122
South China Sea
    Australian maritime and aerial
        patrols 184
    Chinese military facilities 144,
        155–6
    Chinese territorial claims 2,
        11–12, 95, 99, 106, 119, 139–41,
        143–4
    countries involved in competing
        claims 144
    hard power displays 143–5
    island building in Spratly Island
        chain 144
    Permanent Court of Arbitration
        case over Chinese claims
        139–41, 143–4

stand-off over Scarborough Shoal
    138, 144
    US military activities 137, 184
South Korea
    economic dependence on China
        150–1
    Terminal High Altitude Area
        Defense (THAAD) 151
sovereignty and territorial integrity
    defence of 4, 11–12, 23–4, 157–8
    disputes with land neighbours 147–8
    see also East China Sea; South
        China Sea
Soviet Union, collapse 57
Spratly Island chain, military facilities
    144
stability, upholding 23–4
State Council Information Office 97, 98
State Council Overseas Chinese
    Affairs Office 110
state employees
    benefits 38–9
    controls over 33, 34
    corrupt practices 41
    key groups 35
    percentage of population 35
state nationalism 23
state-owned enterprises (SOEs)
    financial efficiency 67, 69
    international investments 79–80
    investment in Australia 178
    number 66
    restructuring of 69–70
    scrutiny of employees 35
stock market, government
    intervention 72
Stokes, Kerry 117–18
strategic engagement with China
    comprehensive approach 187–8
    exchange program for politicians
        and business leaders 188

peak body to advance Australia–
China relationship 188–9
principles 166–71, 187
prosperity 171–80, 187
security 180–7
stratification of Chinese society 39
Sun, Wanning 99, 104, 107
Sun Yat-sen 22
Sydney Morning Herald 102, 107

Taiwan
China's attempt to influence
presidential election 135
China's claim over 11–12, 119
Chinese tourist flows 138–9
formal independence from China
135–6
marginalisation 109
Taiwan Strait Crisis 135–6
Tencent QQ 104
Tiananmen movement (1989) 35–6, 56
Tiananmen Square student protests
32–3, 35, 36, 112, 161
Tibet 148
To, James 108, 110
Torch Innovation Precinct 201n6
trade diplomacy, services focus 91–2
trading relationships 129–30, 163
Trans-Pacific Partnership 92
tributary system 8
Trump administration 92, 153, 158
Trump, Donald 2, 11–12, 156, 163, 183
Tsai Ing-wen 139
Turnbull, Malcolm 106, 162
Two Centenary Goals 17

UN peacekeeping operations,
Chinese contributions to 95, 134,
157, 183

unemployment, youth unemployment
39–40
United Front Work Department 110
'united fronts' 110
United States
Australian investment in 184
Chinese student enrolments
27–8
cyber attacks by PLA 145–6
failure to support Taiwanese
independence 135–6
investment in Australia 184
military presence and defence
relationships in Asia-Pacific 152
military training on Australian
territory 118, 162
'pivot' strategy in Asia-Pacific
region 27, 136, 161–2
role in Asia-Pacific under Trump
165
strengthening of alliances in Asia-
Pacific region 137, 152
universities in Australia, foreign
philanthropy and financial
transparency 169–70
University of New South Wales
(UNSW), Torch Innovation
Precinct 170, 201n6
University of Technology Sydney,
Australia-China Relations
Institute (ACRI) 102, 120
urban–rural divide 37, 38
urbanisation, consequences of 36
US–Australia alliance
and Australian foreign policy 183
impact on Australia–China
relations 141, 164, 165, 182–3
US–China relations
impact of global financial crisis
26–7
interdependency 187

US–China relations (*cont.*)
    under Trump administration 158,
      165–6
US–China–Australia relations 2,
    11–12, 118, 164, 165–6, 183–4
US–Japan defence relations 137, 152–3

victimhood, legacy of 20–1, 28
Vietnam
    Chinese invasion 154
    cyber attacks by China 146
    invasion of Cambodia 154
    territorial claims in South China
      Sea 137

Wang Jianlin 94
Wang Qishan 47, 50
Wang Zichun 119–20
Washington Post 105
water pollution 37
weapons trade 130
WeChat 1, 9, 104
Weibo 1, 9, 104, 116
Weldon International 102
Wen, Philip 105
Western influence, vigilance against
    53–5, 166
WildBear Entertainment 107
Woody Island 144
Woolcott, Richard 184
Wu Wei 116–17

xenophobia 169
Xi Jinping
    on abuses of power 42–3
    anti-corruption campaign 5–6,
      30, 46–9

appeal to cultural greatness 18–23
appeal to ideology 22
appeal to patriotism 22
on Asian security 27
Australian visit 56–7, 94, 114
aversion to political reform 6
censoring of discussions with
    Turnbull 106
centralisation of power into his
    hands 5–6, 44–5
curbing of freedoms 6
Four Comprehensives 45–6
on future of CPC 40, 58
messages sent on first day as
    leader 19
mission as leader of CPC 3–4,
    16
popularity and support for
    49–55
reinvigoration of CPC's mandate
    45–6, 165
on role of media 52
on soft power 101
on Soviet failure 58
on telling of China's story 103
world tour 94
Xinhua News Agency 97, 102, 141
Xinjiang region 148
Xu Caihou 47

youth unemployment 39–40
Yu Jianrong 31
Yuhu Group 118, 119

Zheng Wang 21
Zhou Yongkang 46
Zuckerberg, Mark 97